**THE UNIVERSITY
OF BIRMINGHAM**

INFORMATION SERVICES

This item must be returned promptly

MARY WOLLSTONECRAFT

MARY WOLLSTONECRAFT

from a portrait of Mary Wollstonecraft, c.1791-2, by John Opie (1761-1807),
by courtesy of the Tate Gallery, London 1998

WW

MARY WOLLSTONECRAFT

JANE MOORE

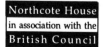

Northcote House
in association with the
British Council

First published in 1999 by Northcote House Publishers Ltd, Plymbridge House, Estover Road, Plymouth PL6 7PY, United Kingdom.
Tel: +44 (01752) 202368 Fax: +44 (01752) 202330.

British Library Cataloguing-in-Publication Data
A catalogue record for this book is available from the British Library

ISBN 0-7463-0747-0   20794703

Typeset by PDQ Typesetting, Newcastle-under-Lyme
Printed and bound in the United Kingdom

1

Introduction: An Extraordinary Woman

In her work, her politics, and her life, Mary Wollstonecraft was the most scandalous woman writer of her generation. She achieved fame as a feminist author in 1792 with the publication of her *Vindication of the Rights of Woman*. The book's bold claim that women were men's intellectual equals, and should therefore have the same rights as them, shocked the majority of those in the eighteenth-century who subscribed to the basic belief that Nature intended women to be wives and mothers, not writers and thinkers. Wollstonecraft's enduring support for the high ideals fostered by the French Revolution and her unpatriotic exposure of the sexual and social injustices endorsed by British law further alienated her from popular opinion. But she became a truly scandalous figure when, shortly after her premature death in 1797 at the age of 38, William Godwin, her husband of five months, gave an unvarnished account of her extraordinary life, including details of her love affairs, her suicide attempts, and her illegitimate pregnancies.

Though her ideas were coolly rational, Wollstonecraft's life was stormy and romantic, a drama of independence and resolution mixed with continual despair and disappointment. Born into a failing middle-class family of English and Irish parentage, she took the courageous step of leaving home at 19 to earn her own living as a lady's companion, one of the few occupations open to a genteel woman. Later, she worked as a schoolteacher and a private governess before gaining employment as a reviewer on the radical periodical *Analytical Review*, owned by the London printer Joseph Johnson, who also published William Blake's anarchic poetry and Thomas Paine's incendiary political treatise *The Rights of Man* (Part I, 1791; Part II, 1792). Working for Johnson gave Wollstonecraft entry into the male world of professional writing. She wrote prolifically, meeting tight deadlines and taking on a range of tasks, including editorial work, reviewing, and translating. Other women had earned a living from writing, but few engaged in the hack work that was the mainstay of Wollstonecraft's career and the source of her financial self-reliance. No wonder that she called herself 'the first of a new genus' (*CL* 164).

Female independence was the essence of her feminism. She argued that women should be their own persons, emotionally and intellectually, if not economically. In *Rights of Woman* she targeted the current system of marriage as the main obstacle to obtaining that goal, protesting that for many young women finding a wealthy husband was the sole purpose of their existence: 'to this object their time is sacrificed, and their persons often legally prostituted' (v. 129). Radical though these opinions were, Wollstonecraft did not shrink in her own life from acting according to her beliefs. When she thought she had found her intellectual soulmate in the Swiss artist Henry Fuseli, she declared a wish to live with him, notwithstanding the fact that he already had a wife. And when she was turned down by this erstwhile sexual libertarian (he drew pornographic pictures and was reputed to have had a homosexual affair), she put her principle of independence into action by leaving alone for France, where she wrote a history of the Revolution.

In Paris she cohabited with Gilbert Imlay, the American adventurer, political radical and entrepreneur, who became the father of her illegitimate child. Yet he too struck a blow at her ideals: while she believed that their relationship was mono-gamous, bound by mutual honest affection rather than mean-ingless legal formality, he flirted with other women and put his commercial interests before her and their child. None the less, Wollstonecraft agreed to his proposal that she travel to the remote shores of Scandinavia. Her mission was to discover the whereabouts of a ship packed with silver and Bourbon plate belonging to Imlay's trading company, which had mysteriously disappeared, along with its precious cargo, at some point during its passage through the Baltic. It was, to say the least, an unusual job for a woman.

Before leaving for Scandinavia, suspicions of Imlay's infidelity had already driven Wollstonecraft to one suicide attempt, probably with laudanum, but when she returned to England and discovered beyond doubt that he had a mistress, she determined for a second time to terminate her life and threw herself off Putney Bridge, her skirts heavily soaked in advance in an effort to ensure success. The suicide failed owing to the intervention of some boatmen, who pulled her out of the water. On her recovery she found the strength to reassert her spirit of self-reliance, bravely declaring that she would not lay any pecuniary obligations on Imlay for the welfare of their child and would earn her own living, as she always had, from writing.

In the middle of this turmoil, she was reintroduced to William Godwin. She had met him some years earlier at a dinner party held in London in November 1791 by her publisher Joseph Johnson. That first encounter, however, was resoundingly unsuccessful: Godwin records in his *Memoirs* that Wollstonecraft annoyed him by hogging the conversation from the guest of honour, Thomas Paine. 'I, of consequence,' he writes, 'heard her, very frequently when I wished to hear Paine' (*M.* 236). In the same laconic fashion, Godwin remarks that he met Wollstonecraft 'two or three times in the course of the following year, but made a very small degree of progress towards a cordial acquaintance' (*M.* 236). Five years later, antagonism gave way to admiration: the two became lovers, and Wollstonecraft's resulting pregnancy led to their decision to get married, in secret.

The couple's antipathy to marriage was well known: Godwin had established his objections to the institution in his monumental work *Political Justice* (1793), arguing that, as practised at present, marriage was an affair of property in which the woman irretrievably forfeited her independence to the man. Wollstonecraft agreed. She described marriage in her first political treatise, *A Vindication of the Rights of Men* (1790), as 'legal prostitution to increase wealth or shun poverty' (v. 22), and continued the criticism in her novels, seizing on slavery as a suitable metaphor for the oppressed state of a wife. Not surprisingly, the couple's capitulation to tradition provoked charges of hypocrisy from enemies and expressions of astonishment from friends. Godwin's closest acquaintance, Thomas Holcroft – also a fervent admirer of Wollstonecraft – wrote: 'I think you the most extraordinary

3

married pair in existence' (*GS* 172). But, despite the insults and the jokes, their marriage was a success, bringing emotional and intellectual fulfilment to them both. This was due in part to their agreement that they should retain the professional and social autonomy that each had practised while single. They continued to keep separate circles of friends and dined as often alone as together. Tragically, the experimental union ended almost as soon as it began. Five months into the marriage Wollstonecraft died in childbirth, leaving behind her a devoted widower and two motherless daughters. Not much is known of the eldest girl, Fanny Imlay, whose life was even briefer than her mother's. At the age of 22 Fanny committed suicide with laudanum, succeeding where Wollstonecraft had not. The fame acquired in adulthood by the second daughter, who became Mary Shelley and wrote the classic gothic novel *Frankenstein* (1818), mirrored a happier aspect of her mother's existence.

After Wollstonecraft's death, Godwin coped with his grief by writing her biography, *Memoirs of the Author of A Vindication of the Rights of Woman*, published along with a four-volume edition of her *Posthumous Works* in 1798. Godwin meticulously researched Wollstonecraft's life and work in preparation for the *Memoirs*. He reread her publications and retrieved many of her letters, though not those to Fuseli, who told Godwin to damn himself (*LD* 289). He talked and wrote to other friends; and when he had exhausted their knowledge he scoured his own scrupulously maintained journal for further information. In doing so, Godwin acted according to his belief, stated in the preface to the *Memoirs*, 'that the more fully we are presented with the picture and story of such persons as the subject of the following narrative, the more generally shall we feel in ourselves an attachment to their fate, and a sympathy in their excellencies' (*M.* 204). The result is a memoir that thoroughly explores Wollstonecraft's personality, investigating her good and bad points alike, sometimes critically, though always with compassion and understanding. At the time, however, there was no precedent for frank and intimate biography of this kind, and the *Memoirs* was received, almost without exception, as the work of an unfeeling husband, who foolishly revealed family secrets. It was the revelation of Wollstonecraft's love affairs and suicide attempts that provoked most hostility. The *Critical Review*, in its issue for April 1798, wrote that the *Memoirs* was 'not calculated to do honour to her memory', and argued that her life should be taken 'rather as a warning than a pattern' (*PS* 342). The *European Magazine*, also in April 1798, called Wollstonecraft 'a philosophical wanton' (*PS* 340); and the *Monthly Magazine*, in its July issue, 1798, remarked: 'It is not for us to vindicate Mary Godwin from the charge of multiplied immorality, which is brought against her by the candid as well as the censorious; by the sagacious as well as the superficial observer: her character, in our estimation, is far from being entitled to unqualified praise' (*PS* 342). For the rest of the eighteenth century and most of the nineteenth Wollstonecraft's name was unmentionable, and her works unreadable, for anyone who laid claim to respectability.

It is probably fair to say that Wollstonecraft's notoriety at this period was more emblematic than individual. When Britain declared war on France in 1793, all the orthodox forces of intellectual debate were marshalled for a lengthy campaign of attack on revolutionary ideals; and, in a paradoxical sense, the ultimate compliment paid to Wollstonecraft's radicalism was the amount of derision she attracted. Conversely, there were some eloquent testimonies to her heroism; these came mostly from men, especially poets. Blake, Coleridge, and Wordsworth all wrote poems to or about her.[1] Even so, for many women readers Wollstonecraft's name was too sullied by charges of sexual misconduct for her work to be taken seriously. Only at the end of the nineteenth century, when radical ideas began to be discussed once more in intellectual circles, did her writing become a force to be reckoned with.

What kind of books did this extraordinary woman write, and how did her ideas evolve over the ten years of her career? As a professional author, Wollstonecraft produced a substantial body of work that ranged across a wide variety of genres. Fiction, history, political treatises, translations from French and German, travel writing, and works of education were all within her grasp. Yet, in spite of this diversity, and notwithstanding the publication in 1989 of a seven-volume edition of the complete works, assessments of Wollstonecraft's *œuvre* have almost invariably focused on *Vindication of the Rights of Woman*. The reason why this is the book that has caught the attention of the majority of Wollstonecraft's readers lies in the probing questions it raises about every aspect of women's lives, from marriage, maternity, and sexual conduct, on the one hand, to education, employment, and political rights, on the other. Are men naturally promiscuous and women biologically predisposed to monogamy, or is this merely an effect of social conditioning? Is marriage the one aim and object of a woman's existence, with motherhood its inevitable consequence, or can women prove themselves useful to society by other means? And what about single mothers? Do they really threaten the social fabric of the family or the State? Some of Wollstonecraft's answers to these questions are unfathomable from a modern perspective. She approves of single mothers but not of sexual freedom. She supports the idea of the nuclear family and discredits the institution of marriage. But her most original and unexpected observation, one that still has the power to upset contemporary apple carts, is her assertion that in matters of morality the sexual distinction between men and women is unimportant. The traditional and even now popular belief is that the biological difference between the sexes divides men's moral nature and social conduct from women's. The eighteenth-century French philosopher Jean-Jacques Rousseau certainly believed 'that man and woman are not, nor ought to be, constituted alike in temperament and character' (cited in v. 149). Against Rousseau, Wollstonecraft proposed that men and women share a common morality which cuts across the distinction of sex: 'their virtues', she declared, 'must be the same in quality, if not in degree, or virtue is a relative idea; consequently, their conduct should be founded on the same principles, and have the same aim' (v. 94–5).

This was a difficult position to sustain. The reality of the double moral standard asserted itself more than once in Wollstonecraft's life, and in her subsequent works she gave a different emphasis to the belief that virtue has no sex. None the less, for this argument alone, *Rights of Woman* has proved to be an invaluable document in the history of feminist theory. Indeed, it was due to the rise of the women's movement at the end of the nineteenth century that the book earned its current and richly deserved reputation as a classic text of modern feminism. After decades of languishing in the infamy that followed Godwin's *Memoirs*, *Rights of Woman* was rescued for posterity by the suffragist leader Millicent Garrett Fawcett. Her lengthy introduction to a new edition of the text, published in 1890, presented the relevance of the book's arguments for contemporary readers by stressing the need to set women's educational, professional, and political lives on the same level as men's, culminating in the right to vote.

Like many subsequent editors of Wollstonecraft's work, Fawcett understandably exaggerated those facets of the text that spoke to the particular concerns of the moment. In the 1890s the key issue was the vote. The means of winning it was, in part, for women to set themselves up as the custodians of moral values, and thus to cement the sexual double standard in place, albeit for the same reasons that Wollstonecraft wished to see it abolished. But in the 1970s, when the second tidal wave of feminism swept across Europe and America, it was women's demand to enjoy the same sexual freedom as men, unhampered by an outdated and sexist morality, that dominated debate. Here again, editors of *Rights of Woman* approached the text from the perspective of present concerns. The decade's preoccupation with sexual liberation led one editor, Miriam Brody, to warn readers that they 'may find a few of the pronouncements the *Vindication* makes on marriage and motherhood frankly surprising.' "The neglected wife is, in general, the best mother" is one sober suggestion, and "an unhappy marriage is often very advantageous to the family" another'.[2] In the 1980s and 1990s, however, the climate changed again and recent critics have focused their attention on history, judging Wollstonecraft's work less in the light of current interests than in the historical and cultural context of her own moment. At the end of the twentieth century the overriding importance of *Rights of Woman* in Wollstonecraft's *œuvre* is beyond dispute. That it has furnished generations of readers with material for debate is sufficient testimony to its power. Yet Wollstonecraft is a much more fascinating figure, her life far richer, and the impact of that life on her ideas a great deal stronger than an account of one work alone can convey.

All Wollstonecraft's books are intensely self-revealing; she continually wrote out of her experience of life, and sometimes in opposition to it, but never in isolation from it. This trait is most pronounced in *Letters Written During a Short Residence in Sweden, Norway and Denmark* (1796), where she announces: 'I found I could not avoid being continually the first person – "the little hero of each tale"' (vi. 241). But it also appears in her early works, *Thoughts on the Education of Daughters* (1787), which emerged from her revolt against her own family's values, and *Original Stories from Real Life* (1788), in which she stars thinly disguised as the incomparably moral Mrs Mason, who overturns the sexual prejudices of the time by insisting on the importance of providing even wealthy girls with an education in reason. It is this investment of herself in her writing that makes Wollstonecraft such an exciting author to read. Extraordinary and painful as her life sometimes was, she never sought release from its complications in the comfort of abstract reasoning; on the contrary, by bringing her experiences to bear on her work, she continually modified her theoretical views. Virginia Woolf saw and admired this quality. In her short essay 'Mary Wollstonecraft', published in 1932, Woolf wrote: 'Every day she made theories by which life should be lived; and every day she came smack against the rock of other people's prejudices. Every day too – for she was no pedant, no cold-blooded theorist – something was born in her that thrust aside her theories and forced her to model them afresh.'[3]

Only by reading the range of Wollstonecraft's writing is it possible to get the measure of that remodelling and to trace the tensions and contradictions that led up to and continued beyond *Rights of Woman*. What is revealed, in consequence, is a series of works that do not merely explain, but also explore and seek to change the terrain of sexual politics in eighteenth-century England.

2

Early Rebellion:
Thoughts on the Education of Daughters, *Mary. A Fiction,* and 'The Cave of Fancy'

Wollstonecraft's radicalism lay in her ability to write to the moment, to tap into the concerns of the day, but also to complicate them in ways that raised new questions about her culture's beliefs. Her first publication was *Thoughts on the Education of Daughters: with Reflections on Female Conduct, in the More Important Duties of Life* (1787). She wrote it in six weeks and sold it to the publisher Joseph Johnson for ten guineas. Female education was a shrewd choice for a new author to work on, especially a female author, for it was one of the few areas of intellectual debate in which women were taken seriously, both as readers and writers. Educational and conduct books of the previous century had been written by, about, and for aristocratic gentlemen, but in Wollstonecraft's epoch a new group of middle-class writers, many of them women, specialized in works of domestic instruction intended for female readers. This gender shift had its origin in the cultural revolution that transformed the economic, social, and sexual relations of eighteenth-century English life: the rise of professional men – doctors, lawyers, bankers, industrialists, and shopkeepers – meant that for the first time in England there existed a powerful class outside the aristocracy that had the wealth to keep wives and daughters at home. We thus begin to see the emergence in this period of a domestic ideology that identified the private space of home as woman's proper sphere; in the nineteenth century this led to the unique placement of women at the moral centre of family life, but in the eighteenth, as Wollstonecraft was to observe, the cult of domesticity made them little more than ornamental dolls: fragile, flirtatious, and helpless.

Since upper- and middle-class girls were destined for domesticity, it was not anticipated that a girl would benefit from an intellectual education. On the contrary, moralists concurred that too much learning stood to ruin her chances of making the greatly desired good marriage. Reading, writing, and arithmetic were obviously important, but the bulk of her education would be directed towards domestic achievements, such as speaking French, painting watercolours, or playing parlour music – accomplishments that would serve her well on the marriage market. Any sign of an independent intellect, on the other hand, could prove a positive hindrance. Dr Gregory, author of a popular conduct manual entitled *A Father's Legacy to his Daughters* (1774), a book that Wollstonecraft later attacked in *Rights of Woman*, warns young women thus:

> Be even cautious in displaying your good sense. It will be thought you assume a superiority over the rest of the company – But if you happen to have any learning, keep it a profound secret, especially from the men who generally look with a jealous and malignant eye on a woman of great parts, and a cultivated understanding.   (cited in v. 167–8)

Behind Gregory's words lay the belief that Nature had made women different from men in mind as well as in body, thus fitting them for distinct social roles. Women's innate modesty, pliancy, and weakness (said the men) suited them to home life; just as men's powerful intellects enabled them to excel in the public world of business, scholarship, and politics.

Mary Wollstonecraft stood almost alone in arguing otherwise. Though *Education of Daughters* is derivative from the traditional conduct book in so far as it includes the standard topics of dress, manners, morals, love, marriage, the treatment of servants, and the fine arts, it presents arguments that are far from conventional, making the book as a whole significantly more radical than its format suggests. What we see in *Education of Daughters* is Wollstonecraft appropriating the genre of conduct literature for the transmission of feminist opinions, so that the content of the book pushes in mutinous fashion against the restrictions of its form. Her later works are full of instances of this kind of formal subversion, but that she should be so adventurous in a publication that was not only her first, but was also written in order to generate an income and might therefore have easily pandered to popular opinion, gives an early indication of how radical a writer she was.

The section on 'Reading' provides a clear example of the challenge *Education of Daughters* poses to accepted beliefs. Where other authors advised girls to suppress their intellectual curiosity, reading only as much as is necessary for polite conversation, Wollstonecraft urges them to read widely and think independently:

> I would have every one try to form an opinion of an author themselves, though modesty may restrain them from mentioning it. Many are so anxious to have the reputation of taste, that they only praise the authors whose merit is indisputable. I am sick of hearing of the sublimity of Milton, the elegance and harmony of Pope, and the original, untaught genius of Shakespear [*sic*]. (iv. 21)

Although the reference to the restraint of 'modesty' nods in the direction of feminine propriety, the overall effect of this passage is to persuade us that women are not innately inferior in intellect to men; it is rather that men, and society in general, encourage them to be conformist, to fall in line with reigning critical opinion. It is striking, too, that Wollstonecraft asserts her convictions in the first person; this is more than a stylistic quirk: it focuses attention on the individuality of her thought and, by implication, testifies to the authority of a female intellect. In fact, she was to employ this device of speaking in the first person in her major theoretical works, *Rights of Men* and *Rights of Woman*, which rarely bow to the prejudices of established authors. This is not to say that Wollstonecraft was not swayed by existing ideas. Her biggest debts were to Rousseau and to the seventeenth-century English philosopher John Locke.[1] None the less, there is something of the autodidact about her, which finds constant expression in the rebelliousness of her prose. As we shall see when we examine *Mary. A Fiction*, not even Rousseau, her mentor, could command total allegiance.

Writing in the first person also enabled Wollstonecraft, of course, to put a personal spin on her reflections, and this too is significant for any appraisal of her work. It is the fusion of individual experience and philosophical thought that gives her writing its polemical edge. This is particularly apparent in her discussions of love, romance, and matrimony, in which she draws on the harrowing details of her own experience in order to make a general statement about the oppression of women. Remarkably for a work of conduct, the section on 'Matrimony' is full of negative insights. Reassuring pictures of cosy domesticity are not provided; there are no portraits of adoring husbands, happy wives, and beatifically smiling children. Instead, the section opens with the observation: 'Early marriages are, in my opinion, a stop to improvement. If we were born only "to draw nutrition, propagate and rot," the sooner the end of creation was answered the better; but as women are here allowed to have souls, the soul ought to be attended to' (iv. 31). The objection is shockingly clear: marriage reduces a girl to her animal function, to the role of brood mare. 'Nothing', Wollstonecraft goes on to argue, 'calls forth the faculties so much as the being obliged to struggle with the world; and this is not a woman's province in a married state' (iv. 32). It is true that even conservative manuals, such as Dr Gregory's *Legacy*, cautioned girls against harbouring unrealistic expectations of married life, especially that of hoping to find the lover in the husband, but rarely did they attack the institution or structure of marriage itself, and certainly not in Wollstonecraft's unremittingly harsh terms.

But then in 1786, when she was writing her book, Wollstonecraft had little reason to celebrate the institution of marriage. She had slept on the landing as a young girl to prevent her violent father from thrashing her mother, and had seen her recently married sister Eliza bite her wedding ring in a frenzy of postnatal depression. In fact, she had been instrumental in organizing Eliza's escape from her husband, whom Eliza implied had been misusing her.[2] Wollstonecraft's intervention further alienated her from her elder brother, Ned, a qualified attorney, who upheld the legal view that no woman had the right to leave a husband without his consent. In later years, Eliza also turned against Wollstonecraft, blaming her for destroying a union that had barely had a chance to establish itself (*LD* 42).

Wollstonecraft's private life during the years 1780–5 was no less disappointing than her family one. In 1785 her close friend Fanny Blood, whom she had met when she was 16 and loved ever since, left England to marry in Lisbon, leaving Wollstonecraft feeling abandoned and alone. She wrote to Fanny's brother, George, 'without some one to love This world [as opposed to the afterlife] is a desart [*sic*] to me' (*CL* 93). Within a year of her marriage Fanny fell pregnant, and, owing to a constitution already weakened by tuberculosis, became dangerously ill. Wollstonecraft had always thought of herself as Fanny's protector, so, when news reached her from Lisbon of Fanny's condition, she did not hesitate to set sail for Portugal, leaving the school she had established a year earlier at Newington Green, London, to the management of her sisters. Her impulsive loyalty to Fanny was poorly rewarded: she arrived in Lisbon just in time to see her die in childbirth, and her baby too. On returning to London, she found her school had failed under her sisters' supervision, and that she herself faced substantial debts. She was at her lowest ebb, and wrote constantly of her frayed nerves, heavy heart, and huge debts. 'The loss of Fanny', she confessed to George,

> was sufficient of itself to have thrown a cloud over my brightest days – What effect then must it have, when I am bereft of every other comfort – I have too many debts – I can not think of remaining any longer in this house, the rent is so enormous, and where to go, without money or friends who can point out – My eyes are very bad and my memory gone, I am not fit for any situation and as to Eliza I don't know what will become of her – My constitution is so impaired, I hope I shan't live long'. (*CL* 102)

Feminist critics such as Janet Todd and Terry Castle have presented female friendship as a rich and fascinating phenomenon of eighteenth-century life and literature. Castle has written about the attributions of lesbianism to Marie Antoinette, and has suggested, as Todd also has, that powerful emotional (and sometimes physical) ties between women were common in the period – Todd remarks that 'the convention by mid-century was ecstasy – in friendship, family, or love'.[3] With these words in mind, it would be unwise to categorize Wollstonecraft's and Fanny's friendship as lesbian, but it would be equally mistaken to ignore the depth of Wollstonecraft's feeling for Fanny, which is portrayed in the fiction *Mary* as 'a passion' (i. 25). Nor should we disregard the effect Fanny's marriage had in confirming Wollstonecraft's view of herself as one bound to be disappointed in love, not least because it is this kind of personal defeat that Wollstonecraft attempts to get to grips with in *Education of*

Daughters. For example, in a section entitled 'The Benefits Which Arise from Disappointments', she asserts: 'In the school of adversity we learn knowledge as well as virtue; yet we lament our hard fate, dwell on our disappointments, and never consider that our own wayward minds, and inconsistent hearts, require these needful correctives. Medicines are not sent to persons in health' (iv. 36). She continues: 'I have often thought it might be set down as a maxim, that the greatest disappointment we can meet with is the gratification of our fondest wishes' (iv. 36). It may seem contradictory to encounter such quasi-religious resignation in a text that I have introduced as feminist, but it is important to be aware of this aspect of Wollstonecraft's life and work, for it provides the basis for understanding the complex network of emotions around which she weaves her feminism.[4] By the same token, it also complicates any reading of her feminism as straightforward polemic, pushing unerringly towards the goal of female independence.

Fanny was not Wollstonecraft's first or only setback. She had felt the keen sting of rejection some years earlier, in the late 1770s, when she was employed as a lady's companion in Bath. Here she was courted for a brief while by Joshua Waterhouse, a handsome but snobbish Cambridge don – too snobbish it seems to make any firm commitment to someone as low down the scale of middle-class gentility as Wollstonecraft. Then there was her friendship with John Hewlett, a fellow schoolteacher whom she met at Newington Green in the mid-1780s. Hewlett admired her: he arranged for publication of *Education of Daughters* with Joseph Johnson, and thought her impressive enough to introduce to the aged but still mighty Dr Johnson.[5] And Wollstonecraft thought Hewlett, or 'poor Hewlett', as she called him after his marriage, worthy of comparison to Rousseau (*CL* 145). Of Hewlett's wife, she remarked, 'how he is yoked!' (*CL* 115); and of herself, she wrote plaintively, 'I am too apt to be attached with a degree of warmth that is not consistent with a probationary state, I have leaned on earth and have been *sorely hurt*' (*CL* 105).[6]

All this pain and rejection finds its way into *Education of Daughters*. Wollstonecraft writes with conviction about the injustices suffered by her sex in general, and still more so about the plight of women like herself. In a section entitled

'Unfortunate Situation of Females, Fashionably Educated, and Left Without a Fortune' (iv. 25), which has no comparison in the run of conduct books, Wollstonecraft protests at the fate of sensitive and intelligent women, who are denied a meaningful existence for the want of a dowry:

> many who have been well, or at least fashionably educated, are left without a fortune, and if they are not entirely devoid of delicacy, they must frequently remain single.
>
> Few are the modes of earning a subsistence, and those very humiliating. Perhaps to be an humble companion to some rich old cousin, or what is still worse, to live with strangers ... It is impossible to enumerate the many hours of anguish such a person must spend. Above the servants, yet considered by them as a spy, and ever reminded of her inferiority when in conversation with the superiors.... Few men seriously think of marrying an inferior; and if they have honor enough not to take advantage of the artless tenderness of a woman who loves, and thinks not of the difference of rank, they do not undeceive her until she has anticipated happiness, which, contrasted with her dependant situation, appears delightful. (iv. 25–6)

Such frankness must have come as a shock to girls whose dreams of future happiness overlooked the possibility that they might find themselves condemned to wage-slavery and romantic disappointment. That Wollstonecraft knew differently is not in itself remarkable, but it was astonishing that she should systematically reveal and denounce the reality behind the dream.

In the same vein, she goes on in the section on 'Love' – the longest in the book – to expose the sexual inequalities underpinning romance. She argues that because women do not have the legal power to resent a sexual injury or disappointment, they take refuge in hurt feelings, which, through the perverse logic of romance, are transformed into a badge of heroism:

> Many ladies are delicately miserable, and imagine that they are lamenting the loss of a lover, when they are full of self-applause, and reflections on their own superior refinement. Painful feelings are prolonged beyond their natural course, to gratify our desire of appearing heroines, and we deceive ourselves as well as others. (iv. 29)

What Wollstonecraft recognizes in this passage is that women play the role of tragic heroine as false compensation for their sexual subordination. For a woman denied access to the public spheres of law, commerce, and intellect, the part of romantic victim offered a paradoxical means of self-assertion. Despite this recognition, or rather because of it, Wollstonecraft targets the ideology of romantic love as the quarry of her feminism. Her objection is that romance accustoms women to disappointment, turns their lack of power into a virtue, and disguises the reality of their inequality. However, if women were to take a rational approach to their rejection, then, even though they might not be able to redress their unjust treatment at an institutional level, they could at least salvage their personal dignity by refusing to be hostages to despair. She therefore resists the myth spun by the authors of romantic fiction that 'love is felt but once':

> it appears to me, that the heart which is capable of receiving an impression at all, and can distinguish, will turn to a new object when the first is found unworthy. I am convinced it is practicable, when a respect for goodness has the first place in the mind, and notions of perfection are not affixed to constancy....When any sudden stroke of fate deprives us of those we love, we may not readily get the better of the blow; but when we find we have been led astray by our passions, and that it was our own imaginations which gave the high colouring to the picture, we may be certain time will drive it out of our minds. For we cannot think of our folly without being displeased with ourselves, and such reflections are quickly banished.   (iv. 29)

It is true that when she wrote these sensible words she had not met her nemesis, Imlay, who proved the biggest challenge to her belief in women's emotional resilience. But she had experienced Waterhouse's deception, Hewlett's betrayal, and even Fanny's, and it is these experiences, I would argue, that fuel the thoughts expressed above. Although *Education of Daughters* is not a strictly autobiographical work, it shows Wollstonecraft attempting to make sense of her own life by subjecting it to rational enquiry.

The centrality of autobiography to Wollstonecraft's writing is also apparent in her next work, *Mary. A Fiction*, published in London by Johnson in 1788. She wrote it in Ireland during the summer of 1787, at the end of a brief stint as governess to the children of Lord and Lady Kingsborough, the richest landowners in the country. Only duty could force her to take the post, she told Fanny's brother, yet the collapse of her school had plunged her into a debt of 'near eighty or ninety pounds' (*CL* 111), and, since Lady Kingsborough had promised her a yearly salary of forty pounds (*CL* 110), she had little option but to resign herself to servitude. In the event, she did not last a full calendar year, and was dismissed from her post in August 1787. To judge from Wollstonecraft's letters, it seems that Lady Kingsborough found her opinionated and argumentative. Even so, Wollstonecraft admits to being treated better than she had anticipated – she was invited to attend her employer's soirées, for example – but as time went on a rivalry developed between the two women, not only over the children but also over men. Wollstonecraft's letters suggest that her dismissal owed more to her Ladyship's sexual jealousy than to her maternal solicitude. On 25 March 1787 Wollstonecraft wrote to her sister Eliza that Lady Kingsborough

> cannot bear that any one should take notice of me. Nay would you believe it she used several arts to get me out of the room before the gentlemen came up – one of them I really wanted to see Mr Ogle – He is between forty and fifty – a *genius* and *unhappy* – Such a man, you may suppose would catch your sister's eye – As he has the name of being a man of sense Lady K. has chosen him for her *flirt* – don't mistake me – her flirtations are very harmless and she can neither understand nor relish his conversation. But she wishes to be taken particular notice of by a man of *acknowledged* cleverness. As he had not seen me lately he came and seated himself by me ... He paid me some *fanciful* compliments – and lent me some very pretty stanzas – melancholy one[s], you may suppose as he thought they would accord with my feelings. (*CL* 146–7)

None the less, Wollstonecraft's time with the Kingsboroughs was not wasted. Seeing the aristocracy at first-hand strengthened her opposition to upper-class decadence in general, and to the indolence of wealthy ladies in particular. It also provided her with raw material for her fiction *Mary*. She drew on Lady Kingsborough's vanity for the character of Eliza, *Mary*'s conventionally aristocratic mother; and she channelled her own feelings of intellectual superiority and social alienation into her fictional *alter ego*, Mary. Like Wollstonecraft, Mary is an intelligent woman – Wollstonecraft calls her a 'genius', which means a woman who thinks for herself.

What makes *Mary* subversive as a fiction is Wollstonecraft's refusal to present readers with a stereotypically feminine heroine in the mould of Samuel Richardson's virtuous Clarissa, or Rousseau's sexy young Sophie.[7] By contrast, Mary is a mixed

17

character: she has a clever and dignified mind, she is 'sometimes inconsiderate, and violent; but never mean or cunning' (i. 35). Above all, she is a thinker, and it is through the description of her thoughts, rather than her looks (which, in fact, are never mentioned), that we come to know her. Wollstonecraft's protest against the dominant ideal of femininity, with its emphasis on passivity, appearance, and obedience to men, is explicit in the novel's epigraph, where she announces: 'In delineating the Heroine of this Fiction, the Author attempts to develop a character different from those generally portrayed. This woman is neither a Clarissa, a Lady G——, nor a Sophie', but a woman with 'thinking powers' (i. 5). Moreover, although Mary is the protagonist of a romantic drama, the plot that unfolds around her aims at realism, rather than escapism. 'Mary', Wollstonecraft announces, is 'an artless tale, without episodes' (i. 5) – in other words, it is drawn from life.

On the eve of Mary's publication, Wollstonecraft told her friend, the Revd Henry Dyson Gabell, that she intended it 'to illustrate an opinion of mine, that a genius will educate itself. I have drawn from Nature' (CL 162). As a character, Mary conforms to the ideal female intellectual sketched in Education of Daughters, but she is also a product of Rousseau's educational novel Émile (1762), which Wollstonecraft read in the months before writing her own fiction.[8] Émile describes the education of a boy of genius, who is brought up outside fashionable society so that he may develop his intellect through sensation and experience, and thus avoid becoming a slave to conventional opinion. Book V of the novel introduces Sophie, the young playmate and bride-to-be of the boy-hero. She is not expected to display any of Émile's self-reliance; on the contrary, her function is to obey and please him. In Rights of Woman, Wollstonecraft was later to castigate Rousseau for his sexist representation of Sophie. For the moment, however, she both adapted and subverted his ideas by presenting a female equivalent of Émile. Mary, too, is a child of Nature. Moreover, it is precisely because she is a daughter, and therefore denied the education given to her elder brother, that she begins to think for herself: 'left to the operations of her own mind, she considered every thing that came under her inspection, and learned to think' (i. 10).

Critics have noted that Mary is not just a novel of education, but is also a romance – a story of wish-fulfilment – that idealizes spiritual or platonic love. Because Mary is deprived of affection by her mother (just as Wollstonecraft was), she becomes unusually responsive to friendship, and yearns for someone to enhance her being and cure her alienation. So anxious is Mary to win her mother's love that she agrees, at her mother's dying request, to an arranged marriage with Charles, a typical young gallant whom she hardly knows. Mary is grimly aware that she neither loves nor cares for Charles; furthermore, she has already chosen a life partner in her friend, Ann. 'She loved Ann better than any one in the world – to snatch her from the very jaws of destruction – she would have encountered a lion. To have this friend constantly with her; to make her mind easy with respect to her family, would it not be superlative bliss?' (i. 20).[9] In the event, Charles departs for the continent immediately after the wedding, leaving his marriage unconsummated, and releasing Mary to travel to Lisbon with Ann in search of relief for her friend's consumptive condition. Godwin writes in his *Memoirs* that a 'considerable part of this story consists, with certain modifications, of the incidents of [Wollstonecraft's] own friendship with Fanny' (M. 223). In Lisbon, Mary forms a spiritual and intellectual attachment with Henry (bringing to mind Wollstonecraft's association with Hewlett). In spite of their mutual closeness – or more likely, because of it – the friendship does not lead to sex. In *Mary*, sexual love is represented as degrading and divisive; it is the ultimate symbol of women's exploitation within marriage, and, even though Mary's husband never demands his conjugal rights, the possibility that he might is sufficient to arouse her disgust.

As was suggested earlier, it is through the inclusion of autobiographical detail that Wollstonecraft creates a psychologically plausible heroine. Part of the achievement lies in the attribution to Mary of unrealistic fantasies of perfect friendship, but also in the explanation of their social causes. *Mary* is a feminist fiction, rather than a utopian one, because it does not pretend that it is feasible to make a clean break with fantasy and romance. Like many romantic heroines of sentimental fiction, Mary is the victim of an overactive imagination. Her desires cannot be fulfilled in patriarchal society, and this is why they are at once seductive and dangerous. It is not unusual to encounter frustrated female longing in sentimental fiction of the time, but, while a traditional novel might present female distress as a mere given, with *Mary* we see a woman struggling to understand her emotional anguish. To convey Mary's troubled inner self, Wollstonecraft experiments with free indirect discourse, described by Gary Kelly as the 'relatively new method of fusing third-person and first-person narration' (*RF* 51). A good example is Mary's reaction to Henry's invitation to look upon him as a father. In this instance, the narrator seems to participate directly in Mary's internal drama, to share in her confusion, rather than merely to report it:

> He had called her his dear girl; the words might have fallen from him by accident; but they did not fall to the ground. My child! His child, what an association of ideas! If I had had a father, such a father! – She could not dwell on the thoughts, the wishes which obtruded themselves. Her mind was unhinged, and passion unperceived filled her whole soul. Lost, in waking dreams, she considered and reconsidered Henry's account of himself; till she actually thought she would tell Ann – a bitter recollection then roused her out of her reverie; and aloud she begged forgiveness of her. (i. 42)

It is difficult to tell who is speaking these words, the narrator or Mary: is it Mary, for example, who considers that her mind is unhinged, or is it the narrator? Again, is it Mary or the narrator who reflects that to tell Ann of her attachment to Henry would constitute a betrayal of their friendship? The point of this ambiguity is that it prevents the narrator, and the reader, from taking an ironic distance from Mary's confusion. Instead, that confusion is characterized from within Mary's consciousness, which both strengthens the emotional realism of her drama and invites the reader to make a sympathetic response. Another way the passage achieves emotional realism is through the employment of typographical devices and punctuation. Exclamation marks and dashes heighten the extremity of emotion conveyed. They break up Mary's prose in order to convey the disorder of her thoughts. They also point to a desire that lacks a language, that can find no easy expression in words.

The relationships between Mary and Ann, and Mary and Henry, construct what from any perspective is an unusual love triangle: two intimate female friends and a chaste male-lover-cum-father-figure, with the official representative of male sexuality – Mary's legal husband – exiled to the margins. None the less, it allows Wollstonecraft to explore in at least two relationships, or three, if we include Mary's husband, the question of whether it is possible for a woman to attain emotional fulfilment in a flawed, patriarchal world. In the absence of her legal husband, Mary is free to explore an alternative relationship with Ann. Yet Ann matches neither Mary's passion nor her intellect. Just as Wollstonecraft was ultimately disappointed in Fanny, so Mary discovers to her dismay that 'Ann and she were not congenial minds, nor did she contribute to her comfort in the degree she expected' (i. 21). Happiness similarly eludes Mary's relationship with Henry.

As unconventional a hero as Mary is a heroine, Henry is an invalid – a weak and 'ugly' man, but also a thinker. His face shows 'strong lines of genius' and his 'awkwardness' is of the kind 'often found in literary men' (i. 28). Like Mary, he has suffered under patriarchy, for he too has been neglected by his mother in favour of the eldest son. Yet, for all this, he is a more fitting hero for the intellectual Mary than any fawning swain or knight errant. Mary finds in him the 'masculine' intelligence she aspires to, and reflects that 'in his company her mind expanded, as he always went below the surface. She increased her stock of ideas, and her taste was improved' (i. 33). But, although her friendship with him is presented as a necessary complement to the one she has with Ann, as well as being preferable to her arranged marriage with Charles, Wollstonecraft does not allow the relationship to triumph. At the end of the novel, Henry dies and Mary is commanded by her husband to take up her role of wife. As Kelly argues, the conclusion to *Mary* is what distinguishes it from the run of contemporary fictions of romantic wish-fulfilment. In Mrs H. Cartwright's *The Platonic Marriage* (1787), for example, the heroine, Clara, enters a platonic marriage with an older man as an escape from poverty and sexual harassment. In this respect, the novel, like *Mary*, uses the concept of platonic love to protest against the sexual exploitation of women; but it also differs from *Mary* by providing the expected 'romantic' happy ending. When Clara's husband conveniently dies, she is united 'legally and sexually with a suitable man' (*RF* 45).

Whereas Mrs H. Cartwright's novel presents platonic love as a refuge for women from patriarchy, nothing brings home more sharply the injustices foisted on women than Mary's platonic marriage to her husband, which is the realistic counterpart to the idealized, but ill-fated, platonic friendship she has with Henry. Charles, the husband, is not a stage villain: he is neither ugly, violent, nor sexually demanding, yet he repels Mary. She would 'work...do any thing rather than be a slave' (i. 55); she can barely conquer her 'disgust' at the prospect of having to write to him; and she faints at his approach when he appears unexpectedly to discuss their plans for the future (i. 72). Though Mary's reaction to her husband may appear extreme, even melodramatic, the cause of her revulsion is made brutally clear: she is his property. It is to him that she must apply for permission to travel to Lisbon with Ann, for it is he, as the narrator reminds us, whom 'she had promised to obey' (i. 25). At the end of the story, Mary prefers death to life with Charles, and looks forward to her release into 'that world *where there is neither marrying*, nor giving in marriage' (i. 73). By refashioning the conclusion of Mrs Cartwright's novel and others of its ilk, Wollstonecraft, as Kelly argues, 'aims to construct a story at once more relevant to the experience of middle-class women she knew and more radical in criticizing the character and condition of women of her class' (*RF* 45).

Death – not love – is victorious in each of Mary's friendships, offering confirmation, if any were still needed, that perfect happiness is an unrealistic possibility in a patriarchal society which restrains women's emotional freedom. The point is reiterated at the close of novel when the frustrated and unhappy Mary declares: 'I cannot live without loving – and love leads to madness' (i. 68). At once an impossible desire and a visceral need, love is the crux of Mary's individual dilemma and Wollstonecraft's creed of female independence. Later in her life, in her relationship with Imlay, and more successfully with Godwin, Wollstonecraft would attempt to make a space for love in her revolutionary philosophy; for the moment, and from a modern viewpoint, *Mary* beckons to be read as a fatalistic tale. In its own time, reviewers found the novel's bleakness unappealing. The *English Review* announced: 'We by no means...approve of that dismal philosophy, or rather gloomy superstition, which pervades this volume'; and the *Monthly Review* commented that the novel's 'emotionalism' was more likely to enervate young female minds than improve them.[10] It remains true, however, that the radicalism of the tale lies precisely in its refusal to pander to romantic sentiment. Nor should we lose sight of how rebellious a heroine Mary is. She chooses to live with a female friend rather than her legal husband, and embarks without apology on an intimate, if platonic, extramarital relationship with another man. She never hesitates to express her contempt for her husband, and she falls in love with Henry not because he admires her appearance but because he values her mind.

It is striking, therefore, that when Godwin reviews the book in his *Memoirs* he does not mention its educational project, nor its incipient rebellion against received ideals. Instead, he praises it as a work of 'delicacy and sentiment' (*M.* 223). By contrast, modern readers have presented *Mary* as a ground-breaking work: Kelly applauds Wollstonecraft for successfully transforming 'her personal and social experience into general social and cultural critique' (*RF* 54); Todd reads the novel as a rebellious and radical contribution to the history of women's friendship in literature;[11] and Caroline Franklin, in her introduction to a facsimile edition of the text, published in 1995, notes it as 'an early example of a Romantic female *bildungsroman*'.[12]

Mary was not Wollstonecraft's first attempt at fiction. In 1787 she began her uncompleted story, 'The Cave of Fancy. A Tale', published posthumously in 1798. The story is worth mentioning here, because it is the precursor, both in theme and plot, of *Mary*. Running only to three short chapters, it relates the history of a sensitive young woman who is compelled to give up the man she loves in order to marry the husband her mother has selected for her. Like *Mary*, 'The Cave of Fancy' represents death as the ultimate release from female suffering, but also as in *Mary*, death represents a protest against the restricted conditions in which women must make their lives. This protest would continue throughout Wollstonecraft's writing, not least in her educational works, to which her next book, *Original Stories from Real Life*, was to prove a crucial contribution.

3

Professional Works:
Original Stories from Real Life,
The Female Reader, Translations, and Reviews

After completing *Mary,* Wollstonecraft focused her gaze once more on the education of girls. If the problem of sexual inequality could not be solved, at least it could be traced to its source. *Original Stories from Real Life: with Conversations Calculated to Regulate the Affections and Form the Mind to Truth and Goodness* was published in London in 1788 by Joseph Johnson, and it inaugurated Wollstonecraft's career as a professional writer. She wrote it shortly after moving to London in August 1787. This was when she was 28; she had just been dismissed by Lady Kingsborough and was once again without an income or a home. Johnson proposed setting her up in a house of her own, which would be her payment for work undertaken for him as an author, translator, and contributor to his new monthly magazine the *Analytical Review.* The two formed a close working relationship, which lasted until Wollstonecraft's death.

As with educational books in general, children's literature was an important genre that increased in popularity and output throughout the eighteenth century, enjoying something of a boom at its end. Modern historians have attributed the success of children's books to the rapid expansion of the bourgeoisie. The middle classes prided themselves on offering more humane and rational values than the aristocracy. Sensitive parents, ambitious for their offspring, rejected fairy tale and folklore, the staples of children's reading for more than a century, as silly, escapist, and cruel. In place of those works, which frightened children into obedience with threats of hobgoblins, the bogy man, the Devil, and the terror of eternal punishment, the middle classes favoured books that would teach their children how to behave morally and in accordance with humanitarian principles.[1] By the late eighteenth century, as Heather Glen observes, 'children's books contain poems and stories on such subjects as the distresses of poverty, the evils of the slave trade and the need for kindness to animals'.[2]

The fresh crop of educational authors yielded a number of influential women writers, among whom were Sarah Trimmer, author of *Fabulous Histories* (1786), also known as *The History of the Robins*, because the book uses bird characters to portray human morality, and Anna Laetitia Barbauld, the writer of *Lessons for Children* (1778). Both wrote for Wollstonecraft's publisher Johnson, and both condemned fairy stories for being untrue and hence uneducational. *Original Stories* participates in this new vogue for moral realism in children's tales, but Wollstonecraft takes that realism a step further by declaring in her book's preface that it is implausible to expect children to behave morally when their parents lack the education that is necessary to guide them:

> to wish that parents would, themselves, mould the ductile passions, is a chimerical wish, for the present generation have their own passions to combat with, and fastidious pleasures to pursue, neglecting those pointed out by nature: we must therefore pour premature knowledge into the succeeding one; and, teaching virtue, explain the nature of vice. Cruel necessity. (iv. 359)

Such assertiveness from a relatively unknown author made Johnson nervous. Perhaps he thought that addressing parents as if they were the children was no way to sell a book; at any rate he asked Wollstonecraft to revise it. But she stuck to her guns, telling him, 'I cannot *now* concur with you, I mean with respect to the preface, and have not altered it. I hate the usual smooth way of exhibiting proud humility...believe me, the few judicious parents who may peruse my book, will not feel themselves hurt – and the weak are too vain to mind what is said in a book intended for children' (*CL* 167). As it turned out, Wollstonecraft was right in thinking Johnson's fears groundless. *Original Stories* appeared in three editions in Wollstonecraft's lifetime. The first edition (1788) was published anonymously, but the second (1791) and third (1796) had Wollstonecraft's name on the title page (a sign of the book's success), and included illustrations by Blake.

The book's frame narrative shows the protagonist, Mrs Mason, another of Wollstonecraft's semi-autobiographical figures, taking responsibility for the re-education of two wealthy orphans – Mary, aged 14, and Caroline, aged 12. Handed over at an early age to inept teachers and ignorant servants, they display the usual prejudices of girls of their class. Mary has an inflated sense of her own importance, which manifests itself in a turn for ridicule; and Caroline is vain and affected (iv. 361). Two of Lady Kingsborough's daughters, Margaret and Mary, may well have served as the model for Mrs Mason's pupils. When Wollstonecraft knew them, Margaret was 14, and Mary 8. In a letter to her sister, dated November 1786, Wollstonecraft wrote: 'The eldest my favorite has great faults, which I am almost afraid I shall never conquer' (CL 124). Margaret was also fond of Wollstonecraft. She kept up a clandestine correspondence with Wollstonecraft after her dismissal from the Kingsborough household, and in later years she paid her the ambiguous compliment of taking the name 'Mrs Mason' when she left her husband, Lord Mountcashel, to live in Italy with her lover, George Tighe. Margaret's sister, Mary, had a still more scandalous future, one in which Wollstonecraft was posthumously implicated. In 1797, the year of Wollstonecraft's death, Mary eloped with Colonel Fitzgerald, who was already married and, unbeknown to her, an illegitimate half-brother of her mother's. When Mary's father and brother caught up with Fitzgerald, they exacted revenge with murder. Gossip had it that Mary's illegitimate child was also killed, either by her own hand or by her family. In the ensuing court trial, Lady Kingsborough blamed Wollstonecraft for corrupting Mary at an early age. Only Margaret Mountcashel spoke up loyally in Wollstonecraft's defence.[3]

Mrs Mason succeeds with her charges where Wollstonecraft was deemed to have failed. In addition to being conceited and vain, the girls also suffer from a tendency to be selfish and to indulge the moment, rather than taking the long view of things. None of these faults is criminally grave, but they connote an aristocratic culture – the short-sighted impulse to gratify desires instantly, without reflecting on the consequences, is precisely what Wollstonecraft objected to in Lady Kingsborough. Mrs Mason reforms the girls' flaws through a gradual process of re-education, which takes the form of a series of lessons in life.

Rather than confining her pupils in a classroom, she takes them on long walks, during which she relates moral anecdotes and introduces to them people who have been victimized by upper-class greed. The aim of the tales is to teach Mary and Caroline humanitarian values, to instil in them a sense of social responsibility, and to train them in the virtues of self-discipline and charity. The girls learn through experience, and in this way are prevented from slavishly following fashionable opinion. They undergo what Gary Kelly calls the process of 'self-construction', a term that highlights the importance the middle classes placed on individual development through education. In contrast to the 'luxury economy' of the upper classes and the 'lottery' mentality of the lower, the middle classes, Kelly argues, subscribed to an 'investment economy', in which 'the moral and intellectual self is life-capital, to be conserved against moral or intellectual extravagance, indulgence of the "passions" or investment in the merely immediate and contingent' (*RF* 62–3).

In their rural environment, but also in London, which they visit towards the end of the book, the girls meet people, rich and poor, who have variously cultivated and neglected their intellects. They learn that true worth is derived from inward merit rather than from the outward show of wealth or poverty. Claire Tomalin is right to argue, however, that the tales do not take up a neutral position on class. The book paints vivid pictures of the human wretchedness that Wollstonecraft probably saw on a daily basis as she walked about London, and it is the poor who emerge as the 'most salient feature of every landscape' (*LD* 102). In the country, the girls encounter tenants reduced to subsistence level by avaricious landlords; and in London, they hear the story of a tradesman ruined by his upper-class customers' reluctance to pay their bills on time. At one point they visit a family living in unparalleled poverty:

> They followed the woman into a low garret, that was never visited by the chearful [*sic*] rays of the sun. A man, with a sallow complexion, and a long beard, sat shivering over a few cinders in the bottom of a broken grate, and two more children were on the ground, half naked, near him, breathing the same noxious air. The gaiety natural to their age did not animate their eyes, half sunk in their sockets; and, instead of smiles, premature wrinkles had found a place in their lengthened visages. (iv. 445)

27

Although written for a genteel readership, *Original Stories* enacts a quiet subversion at the level of class and gender politics. As the above passage illustrates, not only are Mrs Mason's lady-like charges taken into very unlady-like scenes, but the scenes themselves are described in an uncompromising detail, which shows things as they really are. In this way, Wollstonecraft is able to pass judgement on the class system without resorting to a political vocabulary, which would be deemed inappropriate in a book written for children. Vivid description also serves to enliven Mrs Mason's dry moralizing, so that the reader, along with Caroline and Mary, 'feels' rather than merely understands the need for charity. Such is the case in this scene. Caroline has selfishly frittered away her pocket money on toys and has nothing to give the destitute family. Hanging her head in shame, she awaits Mrs Mason's inevitable reproach: 'I am glad that this accident has occurred, to prove to you that prodigality and generosity are incompatible. Oeconomy and self-denial are necessary in every station, to enable us to be generous, and to act conformably to the rules of justice' (iv. 445). It is through such practical, if somewhat harsh, lessons that Mary and Caroline acquire the virtues of charity, humility, and discipline. At the end of the book they have earned the approval of Mrs Mason, who tells them: 'You are now candidates for my friendship, and on your advancement in virtue my regard will in future depend' (iv. 449–50).

The 'virtue' referred to here is worth pausing over, because it implies something very different in *Original Stories* from its customary usage in the eighteenth century. 'Virtue', as Kelly observes, conventionally connoted female sexual purity, but Wollstonecraft rejects this definition of the term, and uses it to indicate the 'disciplined self produced by reason, in control of the appetites' (*RF* 62). In doing so, she challenges the contemporary belief that female morality is primarily sexual, while male morality is chiefly social. Just as she strove in *Education of Daughters* to show that the intellect has no basis in sex, so she attempts in *Original Stories* to demonstrate that virtue has the same meaning, regardless of the gender of the person who practises it.

Through the figure of Mrs Mason, Wollstonecraft also challenges other sexual stereotypes. Mary and Caroline love their governess, not because she is warm or maternal, but because they respect her wisdom and virtue. Mary is kept awake at night by Mrs Mason's frightening eyes (iv. 389); nevertheless, it is she whom Mary desires to resemble: 'I wish to be a woman', she says, 'and to be like Mrs Mason' (iv. 389). In fact, there is very little that is 'womanly' about Mrs Mason. She is single and childless (having lost her husband and infant early on); she is not vain about her appearance and she is certainly not squeamish: she crushes the head of a fallen lark with her foot, rather than see it suffer. She does not remarry after her husband's death, nor does she cede the responsibility of running her estate to any other man. She takes her duties as a landowner seriously, treating her tenants fairly and according to rational principles. She is compassionate but not sentimental, domestic but not housebound. In her, Wollstonecraft created a distinctly new kind of woman. In fact, she might almost be described as a female professional, not because she has a salaried occupation, but because she applies discipline and reason to her daily duties and does so independently of men. In this sense, she embodies the autonomy that Wollstonecraft was busily attaining in her own life as a professional woman writer.

Within the space of a mere twelve months, Wollstonecraft had published a conduct manual, a novel, and a work for children. Her industriousness and versatility receive further testimony in the copious book reviews and translations she undertook for Johnson over the next five years. In preparation for the latter, she learned to read French, German, and Italian. Her first translation, which appeared late in 1788, was the future French revolutionary Jacques Necker's book, *Of the Importance of Religious Opinions*. As a mere translator, her name did not appear in the work; similarly, her identity as the author of the many reviews she contributed to the *Analytical Review* was veiled by the various initials she used to sign to her work.[4] She also compiled a series of extracts in prose and verse entitled *The Female Reader* (1789), which was published as the work of 'Mr Creswick, Teacher of Elocution'. This was probably a business decision on Johnson's part. Wollstonecraft was not yet famous, and it was as a hack writer, not a star author, that Johnson employed her.[5] Her second translation was of a work similar to

29

her own *Original Stories*, entitled *Young Grandison. A Series of
Letters from Young Persons to their Friends. Translated from the Dutch
of Madame de Cambon. With Alterations and Improvements* (2 vols.,
1790). Again, Wollstonecraft was not credited with the translation. Even so, with this book and with Necker's, she worked in
her own fashion, frequently adapting the original to fit her point
of view and sometimes substituting the names of her own friends
and family for those of the principal characters. According to
Godwin, she 'new-modelled and abridged' *Young Grandison* (M.
226); Charles Kegan Paul quotes her publisher Johnson's manuscript note that she 'almost re-wrote' it.[6] Wollstonecraft did,
however, get to put her name to her next and final translation,
*Elements of Morality, for the Use of Children: with an Introductory
Address to Parents*, published late in 1790 and reprinted, with
illustrations, in 1791. It was taken from *Moralisches elementarbuch*
(1782), a fictionalized conduct book by the German author
Christian Gotthilf Salzmann, whom Godwin tells us later
returned the compliment by translating a German edition of
Rights of Woman (M. 226).

All the books Wollstonecraft chose to translate have a share in
the 'investment economy' of *Original Stories*. They subscribe to
her progressive vision of social improvement through education,
and they seek to inculcate broadly humanitarian principles.
Although the books Wollstonecraft produced during the years
1787–90 cannot be described as revolutionary in themselves,
they laid the groundwork for her *Vindication of the Rights of Men*
and *Rights of Woman*. Apart from the conviction that reason,
morality, and truth are concepts that transcend the difference of
gender, what links the earlier works to the later ones is
Wollstonecraft's attempt to enshrine the concept of truth in
language. Like her radical associates Paine and Godwin,
Wollstonecraft promoted a plain and unaffected style as the
language of morality and truth. In the preface to *The Female
Reader*, for example, she states: 'Simplicity and sincerity
generally go hand in hand, as both proceed from a love of
truth' (iv. 55). In *Rights of Woman* she would make that
observation the basis of her feminist manifesto. Hence the
announcement in the book's opening pages: 'I aim at being
useful, and sincerity will render me unaffected; for, wishing
rather to persuade by the force of my arguments, than dazzle by

30

the elegance of my language...I shall try to avoid that flowery diction which has slided from essays into novels, and from novels into familiar letters and conversation' (v. 75–6).

Wollstonecraft's rebellion against 'feminine' writing is equally in evidence in her work for the *Analytical Review*, which was her main source of income during the years 1787–90. Sometimes she contributed as many as thirty reviews an issue; most were of novels, though she also covered poetry, travel writing, and *belles lettres*. The most striking feature to emerge from the reviews is Wollstonecraft's hostility towards the 'feminine novel'. In her scathing account of one example of the genre, Elizabeth Norman's *A Child of Woe. A Novel* (1789), she lists the stale ingredients of the 'truly feminine novel' as follows: 'Unnatural characters, improbable incidents, sad tales of woe rehearsed in an affected, half-prose, half-poetical style, exquisite double-refined sensibility, dazzling beauty, and *elegant* drapery, to adorn the celestial body' (vii. 82). By contrast, a 'masculine and fervid writer' like the historian and educationalist Catherine Macaulay Graham is praised for 'the very superior powers of her mind' (vii. 309).

From a feminist viewpoint it may seem odd that Wollstonecraft employs 'feminine' as a term of abuse and 'masculine' as one of respect. It is important to remember, however, that, in doing so, she is attempting to break free of the contemporary assumption that biological sex determines how women write, speak, behave, and think. By calling Macaulay a masculine writer, she is signalling her theoretical conviction, which Macaulay shared, that there is '*No characteristic difference in sex*' (vii. 314). The phrase resonates powerfully through all Wollstonecraft's writing on female education. It informs, for example, the section on 'Reading' from *Education on Daughters*; it explains the confidence displayed by Wollstonecraft's fictional heroine, Mary, in her powers of thought, and it would shape the writing of her next work, *A Vindication of the Rights of Men*, a book that decisively broke the all-male bastion of political theory.

4

Revolutionary Protest:
A Vindication of the Rights of Men, Vindication of the Rights of Woman, and The Wrongs of Woman: or, Maria. A Fragment

On 14 July 1789 the Bastille fell; in October of the same year the French royal family were threatened by a revolutionary mob at Versailles, and were subsequently removed to Paris. The violence in France sparked on the other side of the Channel a war of words involving politicians, essay writers, journalists, novelists, poets, and their publishers; no one who put pen to paper during the revolutionary decade of 1790 could remain untouched by the force of events. In Britain those who welcomed the Revolution in its early days included the Revd Dr Richard Price, leader of the religious Dissenting community based in Newington Green, London, where Wollstonecraft had briefly lived and taught prior to moving to Ireland. Price was a mentor of hers, someone with whom she exchanged letters, and whose views she shared.

At a meeting of the Revolution Society in November 1789 Price had hailed the French Revolution as a continuation of the democratic reform of the English political system that had occurred at the end of the seventeenth century, the Glorious Revolution of 1688. Affronted by Price's interpretation of events in France, particularly the confusion of English history with French developments, Edmund Burke, Irish statesman and inveterate orator, counter-attacked with his *Reflections on the Revolution in France* (1790), an eloquent defence of monarchical and hereditary power. Burke argued that Price was guilty of gross misjudgement in likening the sudden upheaval in France to the English revolution of 1688. The latter, Burke maintained, had been a process of gradual reform, bringing peace and political stability to the nation; while the former was rapidly throwing everything into political chaos and turmoil. Burke's attack on the French Revolution came as something of a shock to those in Britain who had seen him lend his support to the struggle of the American peoples to free themselves from the yoke of English sovereignty, and who knew of his efforts in Parliament to reduce the power of the English court. Not unreasonably, they also expected him to welcome the overthrow of the French monarchy.

Wollstonecraft's *A Vindication of the Rights of Men, in a Letter to the Right Honourable Edmund Burke* was one of over fifty published replies to Burke's *Reflections*, the most famous of which were Paine's *Rights of Man* (1791–2) and Godwin's *Political Justice* (1793). But it was Wollstonecraft who was first off the mark: her *Rights of Men* appeared in November 1790, just twenty-nine days after Burke's book, the pages being sent to press as they were written. The first edition was published anonymously, but Wollstonecraft's name did appear on a second, published three weeks later.

Paine's *Rights of Man*, published in 1791 and 1792, is the product of his disgust at Burke's denunciation of French Republicanism in *Reflections on the Revolution in France*. Undoubtedly the most famous response to Burke's text, Paine's book was also the most popular. By 1793 sales of the combined work reached an incredible 200,000.[1] In respect of its argument, Paine's work is very similar to Wollstonecraft's. He argues, as she does, against a monarchical aristocratic system; and he defends and praises the French Revolution. So why was his work vastly more popular than hers? The answer lies in the politics of style. Paine wrote in a deliberately vernacular way that was unmatched by many intellectuals of his time, including Wollstonecraft, who never quite departs from the high Burkean style. His appeal lay in his inflammatory and didactic rhetoric that showed up Burke's language as all show and plumage, digression and no substance. Paine's language, like his politics, was that of the common man, and his book's forceful argument for democracy, for the right of every man to have a say in his political future, overturned Burke's defence of the hereditary system.

Though Wollstonecraft's *Rights of Men* does not depart from Burke's literary prose style as radically as Paine's, and though, unlike Paine, she never entirely forsook the élite milieu of intellectualism, her book remains a remarkably planned and cleverly executed piece of rhetoric. It is a stunning achievement, not just because of the speed at which it was written, or because in writing it Wollstonecraft was trespassing on the domain of political theory reserved for male authors (although these are considerable feats in themselves. Rather, what is striking about the book is its display of Wollstonecraft's rhetorical skills. She turns the tables on Burke's arguments so that he is discredited, both as a thinker and a man; she persistently plays up aspects of his style that point to defects of character, reading wit and sarcasm, for example, as the sign of a vitiated intellect, and plays down certain other elements. Gary Kelly observes that 'she does not meet his detailed accounts of economics, currency and legislation, and she gives much briefer consideration to constitutional history, the events of the Revolution and the actions of its English supporters' (RF 88). Thus, although Wollstonecraft is at pains to present herself as a more impartial reader of events than Burke, the reading she gives of his text is in fact extremely partial, and easily outstrips the vindictiveness she accuses him of in his attack on Price. This rhetorical manœuvre is not a flaw in her text but quite the reverse: it testifies to Wollstonecraft's ability to speak the political language men had appropriated for themselves and to demonstrate the truth of her theoretical conviction that rational political discourse has no sex. Men are no more innately suited to the cut and thrust of political discourse than women are to the language of sentiment and feeling.

This is not to say that specific styles and genres did not have gendered connotations. Not only were all forms of writing strongly associated with masculine or feminine culture, they also signalled affiliations of class and nation. Wit, for example, was emblematic of an English gentleman's judgement and learning, but it also called up images of the French fop, who used his verbal agility to charm the ladies. The fop both highlighted and threatened the ideal of English manliness. Michèle Cohen argues that such was the anxiety aroused by the fop that by 1785 John Andrews, author of *A Comparative View of the French and English Nations in their Manners, Politics, and Literature* (1785), 'could write that although the English might "gain in delicacy and refinement" by associating with women like the French did, this advantage was "outweighed" by the threat to "manliness of behaviour and liberty of discourse, the two pillars on which the edifice of our national character is principally supported"'.[2]

Some of Burke's detractors found a greater source of ridicule in his Irish brogue than in any frenchified mannerisms his wit might be seen to exhibit. John Wilkes, for example, famously remarked of his oratory that it 'stank of whiskey and potatoes'.[3] Wollstonecraft, however, plays on the effeminate and French connotations of Burke's wit in order to undermine his 'manly' judgement and integrity. She writes: 'Even the Ladies, Sir, may repeat your sprightly sallies, and retail in theatrical attitudes many of your sentimental exclamations' (v. 8). But because wit is empty rhetoric with no investment in truth, it is also a powerful and dangerous political weapon. Where wit is concerned, appearance is all, and Wollstonecraft accuses Burke of having 'said many things merely for the sake of saying them well' (v. 29). It is a short step from this rebuke to the more serious charge of political insincerity, and it is one Wollstonecraft is quick to level.

In his *Reflections* Burke had defended the French queen Marie Antoinette to the hilt, finding in her vulnerable beauty everything that was sacred about the *Ancien Régime*. This susceptibility to the Queen's charm is enough to condemn him in Wollstonecraft's eyes as an unthinking francophile and lady's man. She denounces him for being unable to 'stand the fascinating glance of a *great* Lady's eyes, when neither virtue nor sense beamed in them' (v. 18). Still more damning is her insinuation that his praise of the Queen stems less from any genuine respect than from a self-interested attempt to regain the influence with the political establishment that he had lost during the Regency Crisis. George III was declared insane in November 1788. The following February, Burke delivered a speech to the House of Commons in which he opposed the granting of an allowance to Queen Charlotte on the grounds that it would 'create a fund for bribing members of parliament' (v. 26 nn. c, d). Meanwhile, Burke himself was being bribed by the Prince of Wales, who offered him the post of Paymaster-General in return for supporting his effort to usurp the King's place. In the event, the King recovered and Burke was almost ruined. Wollstonecraft retells the history at Burke's expense, making much of his inconsistency in protecting one female monarch and not another: 'you tell us that you have a heart of flesh', she cries, but 'with what indecent warmth did *you* treat a woman' when you allowed 'the feelings of a man, not to allude to your romantic gallantry', to give way 'to the views of the statesman' (v. 26).

In contrast to Burke's political and emotional inconstancy, Wollstonecraft presents herself as the steady and impartial defender of the rights of men. The gender reversal is further established by her assertion that she (a mere woman) will reveal to Burke (the seasoned politician) in plain language the meaning of human liberty:

> Quitting now the flowers of rhetoric, let us, Sir, reason together; and believe me, I should not have meddled with these troubled waters, in order to point out your inconsistencies, if your wit had not burnished up some rusty, baneful opinions, and swelled the shallow current of ridicule till it resembled the flow of reason, and presumed to be the test of truth.... The birthright of man, to give you, Sir, a short definition of this disputed right, is such a degree of liberty, civil and religious, as is compatible with the liberty of every other individual with whom he is united in a social compact, and the continued existence of that compact. (v. 9)

In the *Reflections* Burke had argued that the only rights to which men are entitled are those derived from tradition and inheritance. As he put it, liberties are 'an *entailed inheritance* derived to us from our forefathers ... without any reference whatever to any other more general or prior right'.[4] Wollstonecraft argues to the contrary that the right to liberty precedes inheritance law and the distinction of social class, because it is a right that all men acquire at birth. She also reverses the logic of his defence of property. Burke proposed that the transmission of property from father to son was the principal means of securing family stability; Wollstonecraft points out that the 'demon property' is responsible for dividing the family: redundant second sons are farmed out to the clergy for want of an alternative and daughters are prostituted in marriage. Foreshadowing a major theme of *Rights of Woman*, she adds that the 'affection' which binds husbands and wives to each other and to their children rarely accompanies marriages of convenience. As a consequence, 'children are neglected for lovers, and we express surprise that adulteries are so common!' (v. 23). Here lies the explanation for Wollstonecraft's stand against courtly seduction and sexual intrigue in *Rights of Woman*.

Turning to that text, the central point to emerge from *Rights of Men* is Wollstonecraft's identification of corrupt political and sexual relations with the feminine ethos of the old court culture, epitomized by the French queen. Reacting against the sexualized femininity associated with courtly libertinism, Wollstonecraft's second *Vindication* constructs a conduct-book model of rational, domestic, and chaste motherhood. In Wollstonecraft's progressive vision of a new order, in which women will have acquired reason as well as feeling – 'the only province of woman, at present' – they will 'turn with disgust from a rake' (v. 189). Purified by reason and virtue, and bound by duty to her children, the mother 'no longer thinks of pleasing...Her children have her love, and her brightest hopes are beyond the grave' (v. 119).

As with *Rights of Men*, *Vindication of the Rights of Woman: with Strictures on Political and Moral Subjects* was written at a particular moment. The moment was 1791, the year of the new French Constitution that excluded women from all areas of public life, granting citizens' rights only to men over 25; and the year in which Charles Maurice de Talleyrand-Périgord delivered his report on education to the French National Assembly. Although the report called for free education for children of both sexes of all ages, it disappointed Wollstonecraft by recommending that the education of girls should be directed towards a subservient role. *Rights of Woman* is dedicated to Talleyrand, to whom Wollstonecraft appeals to reconsider his views on female education in the light of the argument she makes for women's intellectual and moral equality and, in consequence, for their inclusion in the 'natural rights of mankind':

> if women are to be excluded, without having a voice, from a participation of the natural rights of mankind, prove first, to ward off the charge of injustice and inconsistency, that they want reason – else this flaw in your NEW CONSTITUTION will ever shew [*sic*] that man must, in some shape, act like a tyrant, and tyranny, in whatever part of society it rears its brazen front, will ever undermine morality. (v. 68)

Her point is that, unless women are given the same rational training as men, they will continue to conform to a courtly

37

model of corrupt femininity and, by extension, hinder the moral rejuvenation of the whole of society:

> it is vain to expect women to spend that time in their nursery which they...choose to spend at their glass; for this exertion of cunning is only an instinct of nature to enable them to obtain indirectly a little of that power of which they are unjustly denied a share: for, if women are not permitted to enjoy legitimate rights, they will render both men and themselves vicious, to obtain illicit privileges.   (v. 68)

Accordingly, Wollstonecraft places women's conduct, especially their sexual conduct, at the heart of her feminist agenda. Indeed, after the initial address to Talleyrand, *Rights of Woman* reads more as a conduct book than a political treatise on rights. Or, to put the matter differently, conduct and rights are brought together and made indivisible from the very possibility of social reform. Hence Wollstonecraft's proposal: 'It is time to effect a revolution in female manners – time to restore to them their lost dignity – and make them, as a part of the human species, labour by reforming themselves to reform the world' (v. 114).

Wollstonecraft directs her call to middle-class wives and daughters – the women of the revolutionary bourgeoisie. This was strategically necessary, because it was they who were the targets of educational reform, and it was they who were most in danger of being corrupted by a courtly model of femininity, partly through the process of social emulation but also through reading novels such as Rousseau's *Émile*. Although revolutionary in many other respects, on the subject of women Rousseau remained archly conservative. Sophie, the heroine of the *Émile*, is described in terms that are barely distinguishable from the old courtly model of femininity. Portrayed as Rousseau's perfect woman, she consists more of body than soul, and more of soul than mind. Swayed by instinct rather than reason, she is less judicious than man and consequently more carnal, more animal, than he. Women, writes Rousseau, 'must be subject all their lives, to the most constant and severe restraint, which is that of decorum...dissipation, levity, and inconstancy, are faults that readily spring up from their first propensities, when corrupted or perverted by too much indulgence' (cited in v. 151).

Much of *Rights of Woman* is aimed at Rousseau's fallacious views on sexual difference. Wollstonecraft quotes at length – and with growing indignation – from *Émile*, using it to illustrate the type of false thinking about women that her book aims to correct. Her alternative model of womanhood bears a strong resemblance to the fictional Mrs Mason of *Original Stories*. Moral, rational, and chaste, Wollstonecraft refashions the domestic heroine of traditional conduct literature, turning her into a feminist icon. Unlike the conventional domestic woman, whose subordinate role is to please her husband – to be an alluring mistress rather than an affectionate wife and rational mother (v. 73) – Wollstonecraft represents the mother figure as an independent and useful citizen. Her radical move is to break the association of domesticity with dependency. She contends that 'the being who discharges the duties of its station is independent; and, speaking of women at large, their first duty is to themselves as rational creatures, and the next, in point of importance, as citizens, is that which includes so many, of a mother' (v. 216).

What is striking about the domestic woman as Wollstonecraft defines her is the challenge she poses to the sexual conventions of eighteenth-century culture that consigned men and women to separate moral and intellectual spheres. Through this figure Wollstonecraft aims to show that women are less different from men than popular moralists and educationalists would have it. It is true that she inhabits a separate social sphere (the home), but that space is presented by Wollstonecraft less as a haven from the public world than as its domestic equivalent. The division of men and women into public and private spheres is further challenged by Wollstonecraft's insistence that domestic affections cut across distinctions of sex, thus forming the basis of a common morality. She argues, for example, against sending boys to boarding school because this will deprive them of the family love that is essential in shaping adult virtue: 'Few, I believe, have had much affection for mankind, who did not first love their parents, their brothers, sisters, and even the domestic brutes, whom they first played with' (v. 234).

The problem Wollstonecraft confronts, however, is that women as they are at present are a long way short of reaching her ideal of revolutionary domesticity. 'That woman is naturally weak, or degraded by a concurrence of circumstances', she writes, 'is, I think, clear' (v. 121). For this reason she is readier to point out women's faults than their virtues – certainly she is more critical of women than most writers of her day. None the less, it is from that critique that we can take the measure of her radicalism. Unlike many of her contemporaries, Wollstonecraft argued that the future of women must not be determined by their past. She does not deny the effects of the past on the present – on the contrary, her book makes it apparent that women's present state of degradation is owing to the tenacity of outdated ideals of courtly femininity. But she refuses to strengthen past myths by reproducing the argument that feminine characteristics are predetermined by women's biological difference. She maintains, for example, that, if women in the present moment prefer the idea of seduction to the concept of reason, the fault lies, not in their genes, but in their education and upbringing:

> Women are told from their infancy, and taught by the example of their mothers, that a little knowledge of human weakness, justly termed cunning, softness or temper, *outward* obedience, and a scrupulous attention to a puerile kind of propriety, will obtain for them the protection of man; and should they be beautiful, every thing else is needless, for, at least, twenty years of their lives.   (v. 88)

Anticipation of a different future is imperative. Wollstonecraft wishes, above all, to see women acquire the status of rational, independent, and useful citizens.

To this end she is vociferous in her protest against contemporary male moralists such as Dr Gregory (quoted in Chapter 2), who instructed girls not to reveal their learning in public lest they make the men jealous. Rousseau, of course, is another of her adversaries, and she takes him to task over his belief that women should not be encouraged to expand their intellects. ' "Educate women like men," says Rousseau, "and the more they resemble our sex the less power will they have over us" ' (cited in v. 131). To which Wollstonecraft replies: 'This is the very point I aim at. I do not wish them to have power over men; but over themselves' (v. 131).

The kernel of Wollstonecraft's feminism lies in that statement. She repeatedly makes the point that it is 'not empire' but 'equality' she wishes women to contend for (v. 173). Innocuous though the demand may now seem, it leads Wollstonecraft to make the revolutionary proposal that the ideal basis for relations between the sexes is friendship: 'Excepting with a lover, I must repeat with emphasis, a former observation, – it would be well if they were only agreeable or rational companions' (v. 169). Friendship is also the best ground for marriage, for, in contrast to erotic attraction, it is 'founded on principle, and cemented by time' (v. 142). She argues:

> Were women more rationally educated, could they take a more comprehensive view of things, they would be contented to love but once in their lives; and after marriage calmly let passion subside into friendship into that tender intimacy, which is the best refuge from care; yet is built on such pure, still affections, that idle jealousies would not be allowed to disturb the discharge of the sober duties of life, or to engross the thoughts that ought to be otherwise employed. (v. 189)

The ideal, then, is to see sex yield after marriage to friendship, not because seduction is reprehensible in itself – Wollstonecraft declares: 'I only exclaim against the sexual desire of conquest when the heart is out of the question' (v. 125) – but because the constant need to find new objects is incompatible with marriage and with the moral duties that devolve upon it.

It is important to note, however, that, when Wollstonecraft writes on the dangers posed by sexuality, she does so not only with women's moral duties in mind, but also with a view to their future happiness. She considers that a woman who has been brought up to expect her husband's sexual advances to continue after marriage is destined to be disappointed. 'Love, considered as an animal appetite', she writes, 'cannot long feed on itself without expiring' and 'the wife who has thus been rendered licentious... cannot contentedly become merely an upper servant after having been treated like a goddess' (v. 141–2). Having no active pursuits other than self-adornment, and no sense of self-worth beyond her status as a sexual object, it is probable that she will be left feeling lonely and embittered by the loss of her husband's attentions. Despite that qualification, modern feminists have themselves been disappointed by Wollstonecraft's message that women should surrender their sexual desire after marriage to friendship and the duties of motherhood. Cora Kaplan's and Barbara Taylor's assessments of *Rights of Woman* as a treatise against female pleasure speak to the dissatisfaction felt by many modern women readers of the text.

As Kaplan memorably puts it, 'Wollstonecraft sets up heart-breaking conditions for women's liberation – a little death, the death of desire, the death of female pleasure.'[5] To which Taylor adds that the price demanded by Wollstonecraft's feminism is too high, not just for modern women, but for Wollstonecraft herself, whose intense passion for Fuseli and Imlay indicates that she 'could no more deny her sensuality than repress her intellect'.[6]

Yet it would be a mistake, as Kaplan and Taylor also recognize, to dismiss Wollstonecraft's interrogation of femininity and sexual desire as irrelevant to the concerns of modern feminism. Taylor concludes that, as long as the meaning of woman continues to be 'forged within structures of sex-based subordination – so long as the sexual distinction is in fact a site of division and opposition – so long must women's sexual subjectivity be a central site of feminist politics'.[7] That the 'sexual distinction' continues to operate as a site of 'division and opposition' is beyond dispute. Witness, for example, the plethora of books published during the mid-1990s, many of them written by men, on the problem of finding common emotional ground between the sexes.[8] We might indeed read *Rights of Woman* itself as an early attempt to bridge the sexual chasm, to find a basis on which men and women might finally attain intellectual and moral reciprocity. For Wollstonecraft, the first step towards achieving this goal was through education, and she devotes the penultimate chapter of her book to the necessity of reforming the school system.

In that chapter she plans to revolutionize the way boys and girls interact, and how they might subsequently relate to one another as adults, by introducing a system of free co-educational day schools open to all classes. Lessons in writing, reading, arithmetic, and political history would be taught to both sexes. Physical exercise would be an important part of the curriculum, as would instruction in the elements of medicine and anatomy (an early form of sex education) in order that boys and girls should understand their bodies and become better parents. All children, she adds, should wear uniforms in order to prevent vanity and efface distinctions of rank and, to a degree, sex.

Wollstonecraft envisages that these changes will teach boys and girls to value one another as friends long before the distinction of sex makes a difference, but she also hopes that they might eventually lead to women being respected enough to be granted political rights, and even to have their own representatives in parliament (see v. 217–19). What is not explicitly discussed in this book are the 'laws respecting woman'; Wollstonecraft announces that it is her intention to reserve that subject for 'a future part', for a second volume (v. 215). In fact, the second volume never appeared. Shortly after completing part one of *Rights of Woman* Wollstonecraft left England for revolutionary France, partly to escape her unsuccessful entanglement with Fuseli, but also to write an account of the country's political history. She did, however, return to the theme of women's legal rights (or lack of them) in a novel begun while she was living with Godwin.

The novel is *The Wrongs of Woman: or, Maria. A Fragment*. Wollstonecraft began it in 1796, over a year before her death, but, although the bulk of the story was completed, the conclusion remained unfinished. Godwin edited the manuscript, adding Wollstonecraft's scattered hints for a conclusion, and included it in his *Posthumous Works of the Author of A Vindication of the Rights of Woman*, which was published alongside his scandalous *Memoirs* of Wollstonecraft's life and work. *Wrongs of Woman* deserves discussion here because it takes in a new direction the arguments made about female sexuality in *Rights of Woman*. Given Wollstonecraft's suspicion of sexual love in the latter work, not to mention its virtual exclusion from her first novel, *Mary*, we might expect *Wrongs of Woman* to denounce sexual desire as the cause of sexual injustice. Instead, the novel turns out to be the story of a woman's 'right' to assert her sexuality. Moving beyond both *Mary* and *Rights of Woman*, Wollstonecraft's second work of fiction introduces the idea that a woman's assertion of sexual desire advocates a political statement of independence, thereby forging a new alliance between female sexual feeling and feminist political protest.

The narrative recounts the fate of Maria, a woman of sensibility 'with an improving mind' (i. 83), who discovers too late that the husband she has grown to detest married her only for her money. After enduring five years of paying her husband's debts, seeing him ruin his health and appearance with drink, and witnessing his repeated infidelities with 'profligate women' – for he seldom looks at a modest one – Maria attempts to flee to France with her baby daughter. Her escape is thwarted, however, by her French maid, who drugs her, and she awakens to find that her husband, fearful of losing his 'property', has confined her in a private madhouse and stolen her daughter. During her imprisonment Maria befriends the janitor, an ex-prostitute called Jemima, whose story of equal and various suffering excites Maria's sympathy, leading her to consider 'the oppressed state of woman, and to lament that she had given birth to a daughter' (i. 120).

Within this frame story of the universal oppression of women there unfolds a more personal narrative of victimization, which focuses on the 'romance' that develops between Maria and Darnford – a fellow prisoner, who has also been wrongly confined, owing to a conflict over his inheritance. In the end, Darnford proves as treacherous as Wollstonecraft's real-life lover, Imlay. This unhappy denouement suggests that the romance between Maria and Darnford is presented more as warning than as wish-fulfilment and it accords with the many negative comments on romantic fiction that Wollstonecraft made in her contributions to the *Analytical Review*. The root of her objection was the recalcitrant sexual conservativism of the genre. Even progressive authors, as she notes in her review of Elizabeth Inchbald's *A Simple Story* (1791), surrender to sexual stereotypes when they write a romance. 'Why do all female writers,' she asks, 'even when they display their abilities, always give a sanction to the libertine reveries of men? Why do they poison the minds of their own sex, by strengthening a male prejudice that makes women systematically weak?' (vii. 370).

Wrongs of Woman is Wollstonecraft's attempt to revolutionize the sexual politics of romantic fiction by writing a love story that employs the conventions of the genre against itself. In this sense the novel can be described as a meta-romance. That is to say, it is in the process of relating Darnford's and Maria's love affair that Wollstonecraft draws attention to the illusions generated by romantic fiction.[9] From the outset, the novel marks its scepticism towards traditional romance by setting the love affair between Maria and Darnford in the disturbing environment of the madhouse, which is realistically described as a 'mansion of

44

despair' (i. 85). Although neither Maria nor Darnford is literally deranged, both are tainted by the suspicion of madness. In chapter one, Maria asks her warder, Jemima, 'Do you really think me mad?' To which Jemima replies: 'Not just now. But what does that prove? – only that you must be the more carefully watched, for appearing at times so reasonable' (i. 87). When, a little later, Jemima brings her a parcel of Darnford's books, she reflects that they come, 'perhaps, from a wretch condemned, like me, to reason on the nature of madness, by having wrecked minds continually under his eye; and almost to wish himself – as I do – mad, to escape from the contemplation of it' (i. 93).

Maria starts to fall in love with Darnford, or more accurately with an 'idea' of Darnford, when she reads the notes that he has written in the margins of his books: 'She read them over and over again; and fancy, treacherous fancy, began to sketch a character, congenial with her own, from these shadowy outlines' (i. 93). The inference is clear: Maria has already begun to romanticize about a man she has never met. She reflects how difficult it is to avoid 'growing romantic' when she has 'no active duties or pursuits' (i. 94), so that, by the time she actually meets Darnford, she has already fallen in love with the image she has constructed of him as a romantic hero. What is more, he fits the bill perfectly. His 'eyes glistened as he spoke, and a trembling seemed to run through his manly frame' (i. 100); 'to make her happy, seemed not only the first wish of his heart, but the most noble duty of his life' (i. 105). But he is also the kind of hero, as Wollstonecraft observed in her review of Inchbald's fiction, who 'makes women systematically weak'. Maria is spellbound by him. She goes to sleep 'recollecting his tones of voice, and feeling them reverberate on her heart' (i. 103).

Towards the end of the novel, the couple are released from the madhouse and live together as man and wife. Once they are back in the real world, it becomes apparent to Maria, and to the reader, that she has fallen victim to the illusions of romance and that Darnford is not, in fact, the romantic hero she has fantasized him to be. Although still in love with him, Maria is aware of a 'volatility' in Darnford's character that distresses her, and she tries 'to eradicate some of the romantic notions, which had taken root in her mind' (i. 176). Darnford, however, will soon shatter Maria's illusions himself. Just when she needs him to behave like a romantic hero, he leaves London for Paris, abandoning her to the 'dogs of law' (i. 178). At the head of the pack is Maria's legal husband, George Venables, who brings an action against Darnford for seduction and adultery. In Darnford's absence, Maria decides to conduct his defence herself; she writes a letter to the court, pleading guilty to the charge of adultery, but denying that of seduction. As Elaine Jordan remarks, the letter, which is read out in court, creates the impression that Maria herself is on trial.[10] Yet, as Jordan goes on to argue, the idea that a woman could conduct her own defence is an elaborate and transgressive fiction on Wollstonecraft's part. In the eyes of the law, a woman would not be answerable to the charge of adultery, for she was merely an object of exchange, an item of property to be fought over by men. We must, therefore, concur with Jordan that 'Maria's defence, in relation to the law and legal practice of England in her day, is a silent and fantastic (im)possibility'.[11]

Maria's defence is in fact doubly transgressive. Not only is it a 'fantastic (im)possibility', but it also gives expression to the equally daring (im)possibility, not found in Wollstonecraft's previous publications, that a woman might legitimately assert her sexual desire as a mark of her equality with men. Maria thinks that, as a rational being, she has the right to leave her husband, the right to take a new lover, and the right to claim a divorce:

> I wish my country to approve of my conduct; but, if laws exist, made by the strong to oppress the weak, I appeal to my own sense of justice, and declare that I will not live with the individual, who has violated every moral obligation which binds man to man.
>
> I protest equally against any charge being brought to criminate the man, whom I consider as my husband. I was six-and-twenty when I left Mr Venables' roof; if ever I am to be supposed to arrive at an age to direct my own actions, I must by that time have arrived at it. – I acted with deliberation....I claim then a divorce. (i. 180–1)

The judge, of course, does not agree:

> The judge, in summing up the evidence, alluded to 'the fallacy of letting women plead their feelings, as an excuse for the violation of the marriage-vow. For his part, he had always determined to oppose all innovation, and the new-fangled notions which incroached on the good old rules of conduct. We did not want French principles in public or private life – and if women were allowed to plead their feelings, as an excuse or palliation of infidelity, it was opening a

flood-gate for immorality. What virtuous woman thought of her feelings? – It was her duty to love and obey the man chosen by her parents and relations, who were qualified by their experience to judge better for her, than she could herself.' (i. 181)

Wollstonecraft's revolutionary reply is that it is the woman who does not declare her feelings who risks compromising her virtue. In Maria's view – and Wollstonecraft's – sexual love is moral when it is authentically expressed, and whether that happens inside or outside marriage is an irrelevance. Thus Maria's bold statement that her conduct towards Darnford 'would be just the same without the ceremony as with it, and her expectations from him not less firm' (i. 177).

In the end, however, the mutual love Maria seeks with Darnford fails to be realized, either within marriage or without it. One of the provisional conclusions that Wollstonecraft sketched for her novel shows Darnford abandoning Maria for a new mistress (just as Imlay abandoned Wollstonecraft), even though she is pregnant with his child. Maria responds to her desertion by attempting suicide. However, there is an alternative ending, in which Maria is reunited with the daughter her husband stole from her, and, after a failed suicide attempt, takes the decision to live: 'The conflict is over!', she cries, 'I will live for my child' (i. 184). That the final choice for Maria lies between suicide or living in sexual isolation with her daughter and Jemima certainly withholds the conventional happy ending of heterosexual romance, but what is glimpsed in the process is the potential of female sexuality to transfigure patriarchal relations.

The frankness with which Wollstonecraft wrote about sexuality proved too much for her contemporaries, and when *Wrongs of Woman* appeared alongside Godwin's *Memoirs* she was inevitably identified with her ill-fated heroine. The only one of her works to break through the century-long infamy that subsequently surrounded her was, perhaps appropriately, the one she wrote while she was struggling to come to terms with the failure of her love affair with Imlay, the lyrical and Romantic – in the literary sense of the word – *Letters Written During a Short Residence in Sweden, Norway and Denmark*. (See Chapter 6 of this study.)

5

Romantic Ventures:
An Historical and Moral View of the Origin and Progress of the French Revolution and 'Letters to Imlay'

As Wollstonecraft's professional fame expanded, so did her social life. The success of *Rights of Woman* brought her an advantageous offer of marriage from a 'proper man' with 'a handsome house' – which she turned down – (*CL* 210) – and a number of new intellectual friends. Among them were the painter John Opie, the novelist Mary Hays, and the poet William Roscoe, who wrote a satirical ballad reviling Burke and praising Wollstonecraft as the amazonian author of *Rights of Men*.[1] Roscoe also commissioned the first of three portraits to be painted of her during her lifetime; the other two are by Opie and hang in the Tate and National Portrait galleries in London.[2] The portrait commissioned by Roscoe, which is the least flattering, hangs in the Walker Art Gallery in his home town of Liverpool.[3] In February 1792 Wollstonecraft was honoured by a visit in London from Talleyrand, to whom she had dedicated *Rights of Woman*; and in June of the same year she proudly reported to Everina, 'my book has been translated [into French] and praised in some popular prints' (*CL* 213).[4] A German translation followed along with American and Irish editions.[5]

Meanwhile the relationship with Fuseli dragged on. But by November 1792 Wollstonecraft had apparently had enough. On 12 November she wrote to Roscoe of her determination to abandon her 'rational desire' for Fuseli in favour of exploring new opportunities in France. She would go alone, she told him, adding jokingly: 'At Paris, indeed, I might take a husband for the time being, and get divorced when my truant heart longed again to nestle with its old friends' (*CL* 218).

True to her intentions, Wollstonecraft set off for France on 8 December, arriving in Paris during the first days of the trial of the King, which had opened on 11 December. The King's execution a month later, on 11 January 1793, heightened the political tension that finally found expression in the French declaration of war against the English in February 1793. War set the stronger Jacobins against the Girondins, among whom were most of Wollstonecraft's contacts. Many were later executed during the dark days of October and November 1793. Madame Roland, for example, the most important woman revolutionary Wollstonecraft met in Paris, was guillotined on 8 October.

According to Godwin's biographer William St Clair, Wollstonecraft was introduced to Roland, and other leading Girondins, at Tom Paine's house in France (*GS* 158). She also became friendly with the English expatriate poet and writer Helen Maria Williams, who had published a successful volume of letters that described in conventionally 'feminine', sentimental language the optimistic early days of the Revolution.[6] In theory neither Roland nor Williams was a feminist firebrand, but in practice they were both strongly independent, not just in their intellectual lives but in their amorous ones. As well as running the most successful literary salon of the day, Madame Roland was commonly believed to be the political power behind her husband, who was appointed Minister of the Interior in March 1792. His subservience to her was so well known that the couple were publicly denounced by the Jacobins, who attacked Madame Roland for her political meddling. She was also in love with the young politician Buzot, and, although her sense of sexual propriety prevented her from becoming his mistress (he was married too), she was frank enough to tell her husband of her attachment and independent enough to be angry at his jealous reaction.[7] Williams, meanwhile, fell from grace with many of her English readers by living openly with a married man, John Hurford Stone. She had been famous in London as a poet and literary hostess, attracting among others the admiration of the young Wordsworth, who dedicated his first published poem to her, but when the Revolution came she sullied her reputation by crossing the Channel with Stone and taking his name long before he obtained a French divorce.[8]

Part of the importance for Wollstonecraft of figures such as

Roland and Williams was their expression of a sexual freedom buttressed by a revolutionary creed that rejected marriage as the instrument of bourgeois propriety, property law, and court government. Wollstonecraft had previously distanced herself from the sexual etiquette of the bourgeoisie when she proposed a *ménage à trois* with Fuseli and his wife. Although that plan failed, in Paris her frustrated emotional longing was soon released by her encounter with Gilbert Imlay. Their relationship was not established, however, until April. Before that time, and certainly during the month of January, Wollstonecraft was unhappy in her new surroundings. The fear occasioned by the King's execution was palpable, and it was thus with a gloominess of mind, writes Godwin, that she began working on a 'Series of Letters on the Present Character of the French Nation' (*M*. 238). In the event only one letter appeared. It is dated 'Paris, 15 February 1793', and it expresses Wollstonecraft's disappointment at the violent turn the Revolution had taken. 'I am grieved – sorely grieved', she writes, 'when I think of the blood that has stained the cause of freedom at Paris' (vi. 444). But she does not jettison her support for the Revolution, and stresses that, despite her misgivings, she 'cannot yet give up the hope, that a fairer day is dawning on Europe' (vi. 445).

Gary Kelly speculates that Wollstonecraft's involvement with Imlay may be one of the reasons she failed to produce any more 'Letters' (*RF* 148). Whatever the truth of that claim, by April 1793 Imlay and she were lovers, and in June that year Wollstonecraft moved from Paris to a solitary house in Neuilly, a village three miles outside the capital, in order to escape the worsening political situation there. As an enemy alien Wollstonecraft, like the rest of the English in Paris, was in a precarious position – she was subject to restrictions and in constant danger of reprisals. Imlay's American citizenship gave him greater freedom of movement, and, although he remained based in the capital, he was able to make frequent visits to Neuilly.

Aged 41 when Wollstonecraft met him, Imlay was an exotic figure who had fought in the War of Independence. He had written two books that exalted the simple, rustic virtues of life in America and the pioneering spirit of the country's emigrants. His first book, a *Topographical Description of the Western Territory of North America* (1792), is in part a defence of the commercial project of land and property speculation in which he was heavily involved and over which he and Wollstonecraft would later come to blows. The second, a novel entitled *The Emigrants*, favourably contrasts the democratic philosophy of the New World with the old.[9]

At Neuilly the lovers enjoyed a summer of splendid romantic isolation. In his *Memoirs* Godwin presents this period of Wollstonecraft's life as one of intense happiness. He describes her sexual awakening as follows:

> her whole character seemed to change with a change of fortune. Her sorrows, the depression of her spirits, were forgotten, and she assumed all the simplicity and the vivacity of a youthful mind. She was like a serpent upon a rock, that casts its slough, and appears again with the brilliancy, the sleekness, and the elastic activity of its happiest age. She was playful, full of confidence, kindness and sympathy. Her eyes assumed new lustre, and her cheeks new colour and smoothness. Her voice became chearful [*sic*]; her temper overflowing with universal kindness; and that smile of bewitching tenderness from day to day illuminated her countenance, which all who knew her will so well recollect, and which won, both heart and soul, the affection of almost every one that beheld it. (*M.* 242)

The couple did not marry. Indeed, Godwin tells us that Wollstonecraft refused to become Imlay's legal wife on the grounds that she did not wish to make him responsible as her husband for her debts. None the less, in August Wollstonecraft, who was now pregnant, moved to Paris with Imlay, who had her registered as his wife at the American Embassy in order to provide her with the protection of his citizenship. No wedding ceremony was held and the legal status of the document itself was uncertain. Even so, it enabled her to travel across France and, later, Scandinavia, under the married name of Imlay. She also signed herself 'M. Imlay' in letters to friends and relatives, though not in her published writing.

Back in Paris the honeymoon atmosphere of Neuilly evaporated all too quickly. Almost as soon as the couple returned to the capital, Imlay was called away to Le Havre on business. In his absence, Wollstonecraft continued working on the 'great book', as she described it in a letter to her sister Eliza, which she had begun while living at Neuilly (*CL* 231). The book was a philosophical history, entitled *An Historical and Moral View of the Origin and*

Progress of the French Revolution: and the Effect it has produced in Europe. Published in London in 1794, it was Wollstonecraft's longest work to date, totalling an impressive 522 pages, and it provides yet another example of her remarkable ability to write in a range of genres. With the notable exception of Catherine Macaulay, whom Wollstonecraft had praised in the *Analytical Review* as a 'masculine and fervid writer' (vii. 309), few women wrote history at all in the eighteenth century, let alone the type of philosophical history that incorporated economic and political analysis along with social critique and philosophical reflection. Such histories were usually written by men, in particular the male figures (Adam Smith, David Hume, William Robertson, Hugh Blair, and others) associated with the Scottish Enlightenment. The modern historian Jane Rendall summarizes the approach of those writers well:

> They saw themselves as 'philosophical', because they believed that explanations in history should refer to general causes, to universally applicable generalisations about individual behaviour and social development, across historical time and the cultural variety of the present.... They traced the growth of changing manners – customs, lifestyle, culture – in what was both comparative history and social science.[10]

Rendall points out Wollstonecraft's familiarity with the works of the Scottish writers. She had included excerpts from some of them in her *Female Reader* and cited both David Hume and Adam Smith in the *Rights of Woman*.

Following the convention set by those writers, Wollstonecraft announces in the preface to the *View* that she will survey French history 'with the cool eye of observation', charting the nation's progress from an initial state of barbarism through its development as a modern nation state, and on to the present moment of rebellion, the Revolution of 1789 (vi. 6–7). By identifying herself with the 'cool eye' of the male historian Wollstonecraft continues the challenge of her earlier works to the gendering of narrative in the late eighteenth century. In *Rights of Men* that challenge was realized in her presumption to write in the 'manly' language of reason; this reversal of gender was followed in her next book, *Rights of Woman*, by the bolder claim that the intellect has no sex. In the *View* however, Wollstonecraft negotiates the gendered hierarchies of language and genre in a new way. Not only does she write in a genre conventionally deemed 'masculine', but she also subverts the linguistic rules of that genre by introducing into her narrative stylistic traits (personal reflection, flights of imagination, digressions, and highly figurative language) that ordinarily marked a text as 'feminine'. Accordingly, the language of the *View* is both 'masculine' and 'feminine': it is a new kind of historical narrative, one whose combination of gendered styles breaks the rigid definitions of history proper.

It is this discursive innovativeness that caught the attention of the book's contemporary reviewers. For example, the (admittedly partisan) *Analytical Review* congratulated Wollstonecraft's 'energy of diction' and 'richness of imagery', while observing a 'solidity and depth of thought' that is described as 'truly philosophical'.[11] Another journal, the *Monthly Review*, also noticed the work's 'masculine' and 'feminine' qualities – its judicious and profound speculations, on the one hand, and the 'vigour' of Wollstonecraft's 'imagination', on the other. But the reviewer added that Wollstonecraft's language sometimes became 'too figurative to be perfectly clear' (cited in *RF* 168–9). Even the politically hostile *British Critic* whose reviewer unfairly accused Wollstonecraft of plagiarizing her account from the *New Annual Register* – the journal of record in the late eighteenth century – observed a 'great singularity' in the book's 'style', although this is noted as a flaw in the text: 'The prevalent fault of it is, that it is more florid than the tone of the subject allows; mixing too much of that of the novelist with that of the historian; the dignity of whose matter very ill accords with tinsel and tawdriness.'[12]

Ironically, it is the negative review given in the *British Critic* that places the *View* in its most interesting light. Read from the perspective of the present, the review usefully draws attention both to the innovative style of Wollstonecraft's narrative and to the way her thinking about the Revolution had changed from one of triumphal optimism in early 1789 to bitter disappointment in 1793, when she wrote the book. That shift is apparent in the following long extract, quoted by the reviewer, which describes the present state of the Palace of Versailles that had remained empty since 6 October 1789, when the mob had forced the royal family to return to Paris.

How silent now is Versailles – the solitary foot that mounts the sumptuous stair-case, rests on each landing-place; whilst the eye traverses the void, almost expecting to see the strong images of Fancy burst into life – the train of Louises, like the posterity of the Banquoes, pass in solemn sadness, pointing at the nothingness of grandeur, fading away on the cold canvass, which covers the nakedness of the spacious walls – whilst the gloominess of the atmosphere gives a deeper shade to the gigantic figures, that seem to be sinking into the embraces of death.... the oppressed heart seeks for relief in the garden; but even there, the same images glide along the wide neglected walks – all is fearfully still... I tremble lest I should meet with some unfortunate being, fleeing from the despotism of licentious freedom, hearing the snap of the guillotine at his heels: merely because he was once a noble, or has afforded asylum to those whose only crime is their name. (vi. 84–5)[13]

The execution of the King; the mass arrests, imprisonments – and murders – that constituted the Terror; the civil war in France and the war between France and Britain; the closing down of the Revolutionary Women's Clubs and the drafting of sexist, retrograde laws: all these events stretched to breaking point the faith of many who had supported the Revolution in its early days. Some, such as Wordsworth, were soon to change sides altogether. Wollstonecraft, however, was not of that number. Even though she conveys her horror at the wrongs committed in the name of the Revolution, her book is an attempt to explain both the necessity of the Revolution and the reasons it did not deliver the rational, peaceful society she had hoped for.

Wollstonecraft's argument is that the Revolution failed because it happened too quickly. 'The revolutions of states', she contends, 'ought to be gradual; for during violent or material changes it is not so much the wisdom of measures, as the popularity they acquire by being adapted to the foibles of the great body of the community, which gives them success' (vi. 166). Expanding this thesis, she argues that the pace of change was too swift in France to allow the members of the new National Assembly, and the people in general, time to distance themselves from the political institutions and values of the past. However well intentioned the members of the National Assembly were in attempting to formulate a new programme of rational government, they proved 'too giddy, to support with grave dignity the splendour of sudden glory. Their vanity was also unbounded' and their 'hearts had been too long sophisticated, to suggest the best mode of communicating freedom to millions' (vi. 166).

Meanwhile the French people were swayed to their cost by fine words and grand gestures. The idea of national character plays an important part in Wollstonecraft's assessment of the French people and the downfall of their Revolution. At the beginning of the book she argues that their love of theatre accounts for much of their stereotypical obsession with appearance and style:

> Their national character is, perhaps, more formed by their theatrical amusements, than is generally imagined: they are in reality the schools of vanity. And, after this kind of education, is it surprising, that almost every thing is said and done for stage effect? (vi. 25)

> If a relish for the broad mirth of *fun* characterize the lower class of english, the french of every denomination are equally delighted with a phosphorical, sentimental gilding. This is constantly observable at the theatres. The passions are deprived of all their radical strength, to give smoothness to the ranting sentiments, which, with mock dignity, like the party-coloured rags on the shrivelled branches of the tree of liberty, stuck up in every village, are displayed as something very grand and significant. (vi. 25–6)

The equation of the French people's historical attachment to theatre with the pride they now take in the display of revolutionary rags, regardless of the fact that liberty is receding from view, illuminates the dangers that ensue when national characteristics are transmitted from one generation to the next and internalized so deeply that they become a source of paralysis or blindness. Wollstonecraft implies that the willingness of the French to be dazzled by appearance has obscured their political vision. In much the same way that she accused the francophile Burke in *Rights of Men* of being dazzled by the 'fascinating glance' of Marie Antoinette's eyes 'when neither virtue nor sense beamed in them' (v. 18), she charges the French popular assemblies of 1789 with being misled by the 'fascinating charms of eloquence' (vi. 164).

Notwithstanding the objection that in denouncing the stereotype Wollstonecraft continues it, the important question that emerges from her discussion of the French national character is how to break the stranglehold of the past on the present. Much of the *View* consists in an attempt to answer this question. As we have seen, she insists that revolutions ought to happen gradually; only by this means is it possible gradually to transform the political, social, and economic structures that support change. The problem in France is that the country's institutions, manners, and morals have not advanced far enough to withstand or support the changes the people desire. To this end, as Jane Rendall argues, Wollstonecraft proposes that the future task of the French nation lies in the gradual development and application of 'a science which involves the passions, tempers, and manners of men and nations, estimates their wants, maladies, comforts, happiness, and misery, and computes the sum of good or evil flowing from social institutions' (vi. 183). Rendall observes that in the *View* Wollstonecraft does not address directly the question of the participation of women in that future.[14] Yet, within her analysis of the failure of the Revolution, Wollstonecraft does offer a manifesto for change that links the future of France to an idea of revolutionary domesticity and conjugality, in which women play a key role.

She points out that, as a society becomes more civilized, it becomes more domesticated. Domestic happiness, in the sense of a healthy national economy and a harmonious family unit, is presented as the apotheosis of a rational, culturally and economically developed society. It is in proportion to artistic and economic advancement that man 'becomes domestic, and attached to his home' (vi. 146–7). Wollstonecraft had already written about the softening influence of domestic affections on sexual manners in *Rights of Woman*, and it is not difficult to trace the continuance of that line of thought here. But what is different in the *View* is the acceptance of female sexuality within the domestic sphere. Instead of seeing sexuality as a potentially corrupting force within marriage, Wollstonecraft approves of the sexual gaiety of modern French women, which finds expression in their hospitable family gatherings and the love they give their children. In many French families, she observes:

> The husband and wife, if not lovers, were the civilest friends and the tenderest parents in the world – the only parents, perhaps, who really treated their children like friends; and the most affable masters and mistresses. Mothers were also to be found, who, after suckling their children, paid a degree of attention to their education, not thought compatible with the levity of character attributed to them; whilst they acquired a portion of taste and knowledge rarely to be found in the women of other countries. Their hospitable boards were constantly open to relations and acquaintance, who, without the

formality of an invitation, enjoyed there cheerfulness free from restraint.   (vi. 147–8)

There is a strong link between this 'ideal conjugality' and the lightness of French women's sexual attitude. Even their renowned 'coquetry' is preferable to the repressed sexuality of the English:

> Besides, in France, the women have not those factitious, supercilious manners, common to the english; and acting more freely, they have more decision of character, and even more generosity. Rousseau has taught them also a scrupulous attention to personal cleanliness, not generally to be seen elsewhere: their coquetry is not only more agreeable, but more natural: and not left a prey to unsatisfied sensations, they were less romantic indeed than the english; yet many of them possessed delicacy of sentiment.   (vi. 148)

Gary Kelly observes that female sexuality now plays a key role in Wollstonecraft's revolutionary vision of the future: 'it replaces both the repressed sexuality of mere bourgeois "propriety" and the subservient sexuality of courtly "gallantry", coquetry and the "mistress system"' (RF 162). His point is worth endorsing, not least because Wollstonecraft's love letters to Imlay, many of which were written while she was working on the View, portray a similar investment in the ideal of erotic conjugality.

Wollstonecraft's 'Letters to Imlay', though not intended for publication, were included by Godwin in his edition of the *Posthumous Works of the Author of A Vindication of the Rights of Woman*. Spanning the years 1793–5, during which Wollstonecraft gave birth to her daughter, Fanny, journeyed to Scandinavia, and made two desperate attempts to take her own life, the letters tell the intimate story of the affair with Imlay, a story that begins with Wollstonecraft enthusiastically planning a future of revolutionary domesticity with her lover and closes with the discovery of Imlay's infidelity and the struggle to find a reason to live. The letters are striking in two aspects: first, they show Wollstone-craft's respect for domesticity and her desire to establish a tight family unit with Imlay and their child; secondly, they show her defining erotic fulfilment as an integral feature of domestic happiness. Integral, because for Wollstonecraft sexual pleasure cannot be easily divorced from emotional involvement. The point is implicitly made in an early remark to Imlay: 'The way to my senses is through my heart; but, forgive me! I think there is sometimes a shorter cut to yours' (vi. 371).

This asymmetry of male and female attitudes to sexuality is a constant theme in the letters; early in the sequence Wollstonecraft makes light of that difference, partly because she believes that much of what divides men from women sexually is the result of cultural impositions rather than biological instinct. It is, therefore, possible for male sexuality to be tamed and feminized by domestic and familial relations. Wollstonecraft's faith in this probability is supported by Imlay's budding endorsement of her vision of their domestic future together. Although we have her side of the correspondence only, it is apparent from her letter of January 1794 that he gave her reason to assume he shared her dream of family life:

> What a picture you have sketched of our fire-side! Yes, my love, my fancy was instantly at work, and I found my head on your shoulder, whilst my eyes were fixed on the little creatures that were clinging about your knees. I did not absolutely determine that there should be six – if you have not set your heart on this round number. (vi. 380)

Yet as the letters continue the possibility of this vision coming to pass begins to look extremely doubtful. There was a brief period of tranquillity: in February 1794 Wollstonecraft tired of waiting for Imlay to return to Paris and joined him at Le Havre. On 14 May she gave birth to their daughter, and for a short while the three lived together as a family. In August, however, Imlay was called away again, this time to London, and Wollstonecraft returned to Paris to be near friends. At first she wrote affectionate letters in anticipation of his early return, but for the next seven months Imlay shilly-shallied so much that Wollstonecraft could never be certain when she would next see him. By December she began to rebel and wrote a defensive letter, affirming her intention to 'live without your assistance' and to support Fanny herself. She denounces in prophetic vein the 'common run of men', to whose number Imlay would soon show himself to belong, for supposing 'the wife, slave rather, whom they maintain, has no right to complain' (vi. 396). Fully assuming that right, Wollstonecraft reminds him that there is a distinction between fidelity and constancy, 'and such a degree of respect do I think due to myself, that if only probity, which is a good thing in its place, brings you back, never return!' (vi. 396).

In spite of these brave words, by the following February, when Imlay had still not returned, Wollstonecraft felt her world collapse. Harbouring suicidal thoughts, she confessed: 'I am sick at heart; and, but for this little darling [Fanny] I would cease to care about a life, which is now stripped of every charm' (vi. 400). She had by now given Imlay the power of life and death, yet she struggled to assert her independence in the face of despair, frequently remarking that if his affection was gone, she did not wish for his money: 'I would sooner submit to menial service', she wrote (vi. 401). Even so, her hopes were raised when she received word from him in early April 1795 suggesting that she join him in London.

She did as he requested. To judge from the attempt she made on her life shortly after her arrival in London, it seems plain that the reconciliation did not turn out as planned. Two months later she agreed to travel to Scandinavia to conduct business on Imlay's behalf. But she was far from happy about his absorption in commerce, which she blamed for his hard-heartedness and his 'satiety' (vi. 408). A bleak and accusatory letter written from Hull while awaiting her ship suggests that in the final instance Imlay's sexuality was not, after all, open to transformation. As the affair neared its bitter end, the sexual difference that Wollstonecraft had jokingly alluded to at the beginning of the relationship widened into an unbridgeable gulf. Pointing to the contrast between her domesticated sexuality and his promiscuity, she reproaches him thus:

> Ah! my friend, you know not the ineffable delight, the exquisite pleasure, which arises from a unison of affection and desire, when the whole soul and senses are abandoned to a lively imagination, that renders every emotion delicate and rapturous. Yes; these are emotions, over which satiety has no power, and the recollection of which, even disappointment cannot disenchant; but they do not exist without self-denial.   (vi. 408)

Although Wollstonecraft's letters to Imlay record an individual tragedy, the conflicts they unfold between male and female sexuality and between a woman's desire to surrender herself to love and to maintain her own identity have a resonance beyond the letters themselves. How women are to negotiate the conflict between the demand to be loved completely and the need to preserve their independence is a theme that runs throughout

Wollstonecraft's writing. It is the crux of her two novels and it forms the basis of her attempt to formulate a revolutionary feminist sexual philosophy.

Since the publication of the 'Letters' in 1798, numerous readers have observed with prurient satisfaction that Wollstonecraft's affair was not born of a rational desire. In the late eighteenth and nineteenth centuries those hostile to the cause of women's liberation held them up as proof of the absurdity of Wollstonecraft's feminist philosophy of sexual equality. The most extreme attack was conducted in the pages of the first edition of the *Anti-Jacobin Review and Magazine*, published in July 1798, which described Wollstonecraft as Imlay's 'concubine' and laid the responsibility for his desertion at her own door: 'As the gallants of kept mistresses cannot have that confidence, which is one of the strongest motives to constancy, Mary was forsaken by her paramour' (*PS* 344). In a final insult the *Magazine* indexed Godwin's book under 'Prostitution: see Mary Wollstonecraft'. Even two centuries on it is possible to find the late eminent Oxford historian, Professor Richard Cobb, denouncing 'Mary' as a 'silly', scheming, and justly punished woman. In Cobb's vitriolic gloss on the affair, Wollstonecraft moaned at, whined at, and sponged off Imlay, pursuing the poor man beyond human endurance. Imlay then took the only available course of action: 'in order to remove her temporarily from the London scene, where presumably she was making a maximum nuisance of herself with his own friends in the set, he suggested that she might like to undertake a business trip for him in Scandinavia.'[15] Kinder readers have proposed simply that she made a fool of herself over a man unworthy of her.

Yet any attempt to reduce Wollstonecraft's behaviour to that of a demanding and foolish woman is to miss the point of her revolutionary attempt to appropriate for her own sex the right to declare their sexual and emotional needs, an act that has historically been the preserve of men. Wollstonecraft's 'Letters' shattered the sexual silence that eighteenth-century moralists required of women and exploded the myth prominent throughout the next century of docile, sexless femininity. At the present moment they voice a pertinent truth about the perils of love and the insatiability of human desire. The bravery of Wollstonecraft's letters surely resides in their attempt to bridge the divide between the sexes, not the outcome of her relationship.

6

Final Destinations:
Letters Written During a Short Residence in Sweden, Norway and Denmark, and *Posthumous Works*

Letters from Sweden was the last and most popular work Wollstonecraft published. It brought her a new set of readers and ensured her fame among a younger generation of Romantic authors. Shelley and Wollstonecraft's daughter Mary took a copy with them when they eloped to France in 1814; and several young men paid tribute to her, including Shelley himself.[1] The book was equally praised by members of her own generation, especially those belonging to Godwin's circle. Coleridge, Wordsworth, Southey, and Holcroft all expressed their admiration for the author of *Letters from Sweden*, but none more so than Godwin, who read them between meeting Wollstonecraft in January 1796 and her return from Berkshire in March, where she had gone to recover from a second suicide attempt.[2] He later wrote: 'If ever there was a book calculated to make a man in love with its author, this appears to me to be the book. She speaks of her sorrows, in a way that fills us with melancholy, and dissolves us in tenderness, at the same time that she displays a genius which commands all our admiration' (M. 249).

In his *Memoirs* Godwin gives a brief account of the events that took Wollstonecraft to Scandinavia. A mercantile adventure of Imlay's in Norway had gone badly wrong and he needed someone to go to Scandinavia to sort out the problem. Wollstonecraft seemed the ideal candidate for the task, and the journey promised 'to recruit her health, and, if possible, her spirits' (M. 248). 'It was also gratifying to her feelings, to be employed in promoting the interest of a man, from whom she had experienced such severe unkindness, but to whom she ardently desired to be reconciled' (M. 248). Godwin is unsure, however, about the precise nature of the business Wollstonecraft was to transact, admitting that this part of her life is shrouded in obscurity. The mystery surrounding the venture was finally solved in 1980 by Per Nyström, a governor of Gothenburg, whose findings are reported in the introduction to Richard Holmes's edition of *Letters from Sweden*, published in 1987. It seems that Wollstonecraft went to Scandinavia in hot pursuit of a stolen treasure ship crammed with silver and Bourbon plate. The ship and its precious cargo had been abducted from Imlay's trading company by the Norwegian sailor hired to steer the vessel through the Baltic.

How Imlay acquired such treasure, worth about half a million pounds in modern currency, is itself a mystery. Perhaps it was filched from the French aristocracy, but whatever the case he intended to use it as convertible currency for the purchase of raw materials in the Baltic (soap, alum, and naval stores) for export to war-torn France. The operation, which was masterminded from London, was a shady business, at best only semi-legal. Imlay had registered the ship in the name of the Norwegian captain, thereby securing neutral status for the vessel. When the captain subsequently betrayed him, he could hardly appeal to the British courts for help, nor to French law, which had no jurisdiction in the case. His only chance lay in appealing to the Danish authorities, who dealt with all Scandinavian shipping, and this is what he asked Wollstonecraft to do. Her task was to discover the fate of the ship and, if possible, arrange an out-of-court settlement to the satisfaction of all parties concerned. It was a remarkably delicate, not to mention potentially dangerous, undertaking. 'Only someone as daring and determined as Mary Wollstonecraft would have attempted it,' writes Holmes (M. 26). Perhaps only someone as determined as she to prove her loyalty, her love, and her worth, could have.

Although Wollstonecraft's letters never make explicit reference to the affair of the treasure ship, its discovery sheds new light on the tensions surrounding her voyage, and helps us to appreciate her exceptional mettle. The trip was arduous enough in terms of the sheer distances involved, added to which very little was known in England about Scandinavia at this time. The Baltic countries did not feature on the itinerary of the eighteenth-century Grand Tour, and most English people would have balked at the very idea of undertaking a journey such as Wollstonecraft's, especially in 1795, when the rest of Europe was at war with France, making all travel hazardous. Even so, from late June to early October, Wollstonecraft travelled from Gothenburg in Sweden to Norway, crossing the Skagerrak strait over to Tønsberg on the rocky north-east coast. She remained at Tønsberg for several weeks, and went west as far as Risør. She then returned via Oslo, travelling south again; next she sailed the Kattegat into Denmark, staying in Copenhagen, before journeying down the straits to Schleswig, and on to Hamburg, where she took a ship home to Dover. Not the least impressive part of this remarkable venture is, of course, that it was undertaken during the most severe emotional crisis Wollstonecraft had ever experienced.

It is a nice twist of irony, therefore, that it is the raw emotional intensity of the letters that largely explains their success. When preparing them for publication, Wollstonecraft had attempted to take the sting out her reflections by recasting them in less personal terms; but, as she tells us in the prefatory advertisement to her book,

> in proportion as I arranged my thoughts, my letter, I found, became stiff and affected: I, therefore, determined to let my remarks and reflections flow unrestrained, as I perceived that I could not give a just description of what I saw, but by relating the effect different objects had produced on my mind and feelings, whilst the impression was still fresh. (vi. 241)

She did well to leave her thoughts alone. It is precisely this freshness and spontaneity of expression that contemporary readers found so appealing. The reviewer for the *British Critic* was captivated by 'an heart exquisitely alive to the beauties of nature, and keenly susceptible of every soft impression, every tender emotion'.[3]

Each of the twenty-five letters is addressed to the same unnamed correspondent, who, it becomes apparent, has been the narrator's lover. We know now that the correspondent was Imlay, but most of Wollstonecraft's contemporary readers could only speculate on who it was that caused the sorrow they found so deeply moving. Though Imlay's identity is kept hidden, no such enigma surrounds the emotional conflicts that he staged. On the contrary, Wollstonecraft's first-person confessional narrative invites the reader to share her secrets, to become her confidant. The pleasure of being made privy to private thoughts and desires should not be underestimated when accounting for the book's success. Nor should it go unnoticed that for the most part readers responded with sympathy and pity for Wollstonecraft's plight, many of them explicitly welcoming the shift from the strident cadences of *Rights of Woman* to the softer, and, it was felt, more feminine tone of the *Letters from Sweden*.

Some of Wollstonecraft's confessions are so personal as to be hardly distinguishable either in mood or subject matter from her private letters to Imlay. This is so especially towards the end of her journey, when, physically and mentally exhausted, she threw herself almost entirely into the role of abandoned lover. The following letter, written from her final destination of Hamburg, raises all the old worries: would Imlay return to her as her husband and lover, and become a father to Fanny, or was he so mired in commercial concerns as to have lost forever his domestic inclinations?

> You will say that I am growing bitter, perhaps, personal. Ah! shall I whisper to you – that you – yourself, are strangely altered, since you have entered deeply into commerce – more than you are aware of – never allowing yourself to reflect, and keeping your mind, or rather passions, in a continual state of agitation – Nature has given you talents, which lie dormant, or are wasted in ignoble pursuits – You will rouse yourself, and shake off the vile dust that obscures you, or my understanding, as well as my heart, deceives me, egregiously – only tell me, when? (vi. 340–1)

At other moments her voice more closely resembles that of the observant traveller. She reports and reflects on everything, from the suffocating feather duvets used as bedding to the spices and sugar put in all Swedish food, even the bread. The salted fish and meats of the smörgåsbord, the strawberries spoiled by being left uncovered in smoke-filled rooms, the superior complexion of Norwegian women, the selfishness of lawyers and the brutal-izing effect of trade on the manners of almost everyone involved in commerce, the different marriage customs and farming practices: all are described with equal vividness, providing a rich and varied picture of a very alien culture.

Then there are the descriptions of the thrilling Scandinavian landscape – the majestic pine forests, towering waterfalls, and glassy fjords, the clear skies, blue seas, and flower-jewelled meadows – which act as catalysts for her own emotions, releasing a peculiarly inward-looking narrative of the type we have come to call Romantic. Movement both real and internal courses through Wollstonecraft's prose, producing a book that is at once emotional autobiography, guide book, and topographical narrative, and shows her yet again pushing generic categories to their limits.

What emerges from all of this is the restless, enquiring spirit of the archetypal Romantic writer, the yearning, half-practical and half-visionary, to discover the promised land. For Wollstonecraft that place was France, at least for a while; for Byron and Shelley it was Greece and Switzerland; and for Imlay it was America. Wollstonecraft's restlessness, however, possesses a distinctive melancholic quality. By 1795 she was less driven by the spirit of adventure (though that is also there) than by a need to flee from pain. She travels to forget; and, though she cannot exorcize the ghosts of the past, she does at least find temporary relief from her suffering in the sublime and unfamiliar wilderness of Scandinavia.

At Tønsberg, where she spent several weeks relaxing without Fanny, whom she left in Gothenburg with their maid, she is soothed into happiness for the first time. From the cliffs overlooking the shore, she wrote:

> With what ineffable pleasure have I not gazed – and gazed again, losing my breath through my eyes – my very soul diffused itself in the scene – and, seeming to become all senses, gilded in the scarcely-agitated waves, melted in the freshening breeze, or, taking its flight with fairy wing, to the misty mountains which bounded the prospect, fancy tript over new lawns, more beautiful even than the lovely slopes on the winding shore before me. (vi. 280)

There is a real sense of the Romantic sublime in this passage – the moment when subject and object become one, and the self attains a rare feeling of total plenitude. The animating spirit of the natural world provides the antidote to Wollstonecraft's despair: she can no longer bear to think of being no more:

> nay, it appears to me impossible that I should cease to exist, or that this active, restless spirit, equally alive to joy and sorrow, should only

be organized dust – ready to fly abroad the moment the spring snaps, or the spark goes out, which kept it together. Surely something resides in this heart that is not perishable – and life is more than a dream. (vi. 281)

The idea of immortality and of an ego that transcends the limits of the material world would become a commonplace of later Romantic writing; that Wollstonecraft voices those themes here does not suggest that she gave birth to them, but it does raise the possibility that her predicament with Imlay impelled her to explore the farthest edges of her thoughts and emotions, and to find a language that could capture her experience of 'fluttering between life and death' (vi. 310). After leaving Tønsberg on 22 August, Wollstonecraft's thoughts become increasingly gloomy; she received three unkind letters from Imlay in succession and was overwhelmed by despair. Merely to write off her sufferings would, as Claire Tomalin suggests, have meant writing off the love that had led to them (_LD_ 230). So she recorded them – setting down the hopes and fears, joys and sorrows, of a 'sensibility wounded almost to madness' (vi. 303). We might view Wollstonecraft's 'Romanticism' not only as a literary exercise but as a necessary response to a deep-seated need to acknowledge her agony and thus her love.

Sometime towards the end of August she wrote a now famous account of her reflections on encountering the dramatic waterfalls at Frederikstad, Norway. On her approach to the falls she is fascinated by the sight of a devastated forest, whose images of decay seem to hold out the promise of new life: 'I cannot tell why,' she confesses, 'but death, under every form, appears to me like something getting free – to expand in I know not what element' (vi. 311). Then:

> Reaching the cascade, or rather cataract, the roaring of which had a long time announced its vicinity, my soul was hurried by the falls into a new train of reflections. The impetuous dashing of the rebounding torrent from the dark cavities which mocked the exploring eye, produced an equal activity in my mind: my thoughts darted from earth to heaven, and I asked myself why I was chained to life and its misery?...I stretched out my hand to eternity, bounding over the dark speck of life to come. (vi. 311)

This possibility of rebirth in death is extraordinarily poetic; it is an imagined response to a very literal torment, and it marks a striking contrast to the ideological axe-grinding of _Rights of Woman_ which sought social solutions to female suffering. Though the extremes of passion voiced in the _Letters from Sweden_ – let alone the poetic dream of rebirth in death – can hardly be said to constitute a practical solution to emotional problems, it is worth noting that Wollstonecraft's readers, especially her female readers, responded intuitively to the _Letters from Sweden_ in a way they did not to _Rights of Woman_.

Even those members of Godwin's rational circle, such as Amelia Alderson, then an aspiring novelist, found the _Letters from Sweden_ infinitely more appealing than Wollstonecraft's political works, not because she took exception to her feminist philosophy, which excited her 'cold awe', but because she empathized at a more fundamental level with the agony of the woman who wrote the _Letters_:

> I remember the time when my desire of seeing you [she wrote to Wollstonecraft] was repressed by fear – but as soon as I read your letters from Norway, the cold awe which the philosopher has excited, was lost in the tender sympathy called forth by the woman. I saw nothing but the interesting creature of feeling and imagination.   (cited in _M._ 37)

Although Alderson spoke for many of her contemporaries, male and female, it needs to be said in conclusion that _Letters from Sweden_ is not devoid of Wollstonecraft's earlier feminism. Letter 6, which reflects on the 'dependent and oppressed state' of women, is as hard-hitting as anything written in the _Rights of Woman_. So too is Letter 19, written from Copenhagen, in which Wollstonecraft vents her disgust at the sexual promiscuity of the men and the cunning of the women, blaming the former for the corruption of the latter. 'Is not man then the tyrant of creation?', she asks (vi. 325). What is more, she refuses to temper her remarks, even though she anticipates that they will be greeted with mockery: 'Still harping on the same subject, you will exclaim – How can I avoid it, when most of the struggles of an eventful life have been occasioned by the oppressed state of my sex: we reason deeply, when we forcibly feel' (vi. 325).

Despite these declarations of feminist sentiment, most critics remained blind to the political force of Wollstonecraft's final work. Those reviews that did remark on the book's feminist arguments dismissed them as no more than 'the harmless effect of mistaken zeal': 'we could smile', wrote the reviewer for the *British Critic*, 'at an error which is so little likely to gain converts'.[4] The immediate response to the *Letters from Sweden* proved the reviewer right. Wollstonecraft quickly entered literary mythology not as a feminist heroine but as a feminine one – a vulnerable and pitiable woman cruelly abandoned by her unfaithful lover. Coleridge is said to have drawn on her image when he wrote in his poem 'Kubla Khan' of

> A savage place! as holy and enchanted
> As e'er beneath a waning moon was haunted
> By woman wailing for her demon-lover!

It has also been suggested that Jane Austen borrowed something of Wollstonecraft's story when she wrote in *Sense and Sensibility* of Marianne Dashwood's betrayal by her lover and subsequent self-induced illness.[5] Although it cannot be proved that Wollstonecraft influenced the portrait of Marianne, Austen had almost certainly heard of her plight with Imlay long before Godwin made it public knowledge. Her father was a close acquaintance of Sir William East, the man who receives special commendation in Godwin's *Memoirs* for showing particular kindness to Wollstonecraft after she attempted to drown herself. On 10 October 1795, just days after her return to London from Scandinavia, Wollstonecraft forced her cook to confess that Imlay had a mistress. Resolved to take no more, she wrote in her suicide note: 'I shall plunge into the Thames where there is the least chance of my being snatched from the death I seek' (vi. 431).

Wollstonecraft's tide of sorrow, however, was soon to turn. On her recovery, she renewed her acquaintance with William Godwin; they had met briefly in January 1796, at a party given in London by the novelist Mary Hays 'but with no particular effect' (*M.* 256). The following March Wollstonecraft finally terminated her connection with Imlay, but once the news of their separation broke and it became apparent that they had never legally married, she faced social ostracism. Old friends were not prepared to associate with an unmarried mother. Though depressed by the loss of some of her acquaintances, it was not long before Wollstonecraft put her principle of independence into action once more. On 14 April she defied social convention and called alone at Godwin's lodgings in

Somers Town. Whatever else Imlay destroyed, he did not damage her feminist disrespect for meaningless social propriety; nor did he shatter her faith in sexual equality, which is clearly in evidence in Godwin's record of his life with her. Neither partner, writes Godwin, had the upper hand in their relationship: love 'grew with equal advances in the mind of each.... One sex did not take the priority which long-established custom has awarded it, nor the other overstep that delicacy which is so severely imposed' (*M.* 257).

During the day the couple left one another to their separate literary and social pursuits, and their affair remained a well-kept secret. Even after their marriage, which took place in private in March 1797 following Wollstonecraft's pregnancy, they remained solidly unconventional. Godwin rented a separate apartment close to their joint lodging, where he would work and entertain alone; Wollstonecraft also continued to see her friends separately. The arrangement was perfectly in accord with their philosophical principles and seems to have worked well. 'We agreed', writes Godwin,

> in condemning the notion, prevalent in many situations in life, that a man and his wife cannot visit in mixed society, but in company with each other; and we rather sought occasions of deviating from, than of complying with, this rule. By these means, though, for the most part, we spent the latter half of each day in one another's society, yet we were in no danger of satiety. We seemed to combine, in a considerable degree, the novelty and lively sensation of a visit, with the more delicious and heart-felt pleasures of domestic life. (*M.* 263)

At last Wollstonecraft was able to live the revolutionary domesticity envisaged in *Rights of Woman*. Sadly, the experiment was short-lived. On 30 August 1796 she gave birth to Mary Wollstonecraft Godwin; two and half hours after parturition the midwife reported that the placenta had not been expelled. Godwin called in a male surgeon – none had been in attendance from the beginning, because Wollstonecraft, who had written in *Rights of Woman* against the usurpation of female roles by male professionals, had chosen to be assisted by a midwife. The physician attempted to remove the placenta piece by piece, with fatal consequences. After severe haemorrhaging, fainting and shivering fits, Wollstonecraft died of puerperal fever on the morning of 10 September 1797.[6]

Her funeral was held five days later. Godwin did not attend. He told his friends he never expected to be happy again. Within a week of the funeral he moved into her old study, hung Opie's portrait of her above the fireplace for inspiration, and set to work editing her letters and unfinished works for publication, also preparing his own *Memoirs* of her extraordinary life. Within four months he completed *Posthumous Works of the Author of A Vindication of the Rights of Woman* and *Memoirs of the Author of the Rights of Woman*. The hostile public reaction to the *Memoirs* is well known. Even Wollstonecraft's defenders, such as Mary Hays, who rushed into print with a lavish obituary for her old friend, thought Godwin's frankness too much. It was one thing for Wollstonecraft to write of her sorrows in *Letters from Sweden*; but quite another for Godwin to reveal that she was not married to the man who betrayed her. Wollstonecraft's sisters felt the shock badly and claimed that they 'found difficulties in getting situations because of their relationship to Mary Godwin'.[7] Meanwhile their brother Ned brought up his children 'to regard their aunt as a source of deep mortification' (*LD* 256). Even poor Fanny Imlay was affected. On 9 October 1816 she checked into a Swansea hotel, where she died after taking an overdose of laudanum. She left a note, suggesting the discovery of her illegitimate parentage as the reason for her suicide: 'I have long determined that the best thing I could do was to put an end to the existence of a being whose birth was unfortunate' (*GS* 411). Wollstonecraft's second daughter, Mary Shelley, went on to write *Frankenstein*, an allegorical novel about the desire of man to usurp woman's creative function.

After Wollstonecraft's death, Godwin edited and republished in his edition of her *Posthumous Works* a short essay entitled 'On Poetry, and Our Relish for the Beauties of Nature', which had been published previously, under the signature M.Q., in the *Monthly Magazine* for April 1797.[8] Harriet Devine Jump observes that the essay is Wollstonecraft's only contribution to a periodical other than the *Analytical Review*, as well as her first foray into literary theory.[9] The essay is of interest because Wollstonecraft defends from a philosophical and literary perspective the importance of the imagination, feelings, and emotions to which she gave new emphasis in her lyrical and autobiographical *Letters from Sweden*.

What we see in 'On Poetry' is Wollstonecraft attempting to sketch a concept of the poetic imagination that combines her earlier conviction that genius means being capable of independent *thought* (evident, for example, in the description of her fictional heroine, Mary) with her present belief that genius demands poetic *feeling* and *imaginative spontaneity*. An imagined response to a natural scene sets the poet apart from the intellectual, the genius from the copyist. Where the visceral response of the first to the natural world produces new categories of thought and feeling, the studied deference of the second to the realm of the already thought fails to propel the reader or the poet beyond the horizon of current prejudices. Understanding without feeling, Wollstonecraft maintains, produces intellectual slaves, mere scribes, in thrall to poetic and political pieties and therefore incapable of stirring our passions: 'though it should be allowed that books may produce some poets, I fear they will never be the poets who charm our cares to sleep, or extort admiration. They may diffuse taste, and polish the language; but I am inclined to conclude that they will seldom rouse the passions, or amend the heart' (vii. 10). In 'On Poetry', as in *Letters from Sweden*, and 'Letters to Imlay', it is the solitary, perceiving, and, above all, confessional self, familiar to us from the texts of later Romantic poets, that dominates the narrative. Jump argues that this 'new self-construction' allows Wollstonecraft 'to engage in a new discourse, one in which it is permissible to speak not only of her feelings for Imlay but also of her response to the beauty and sublimity of the natural world'.[10] She notes, too, that, when Godwin edited 'On Poetry' for publication, he took the decisive step of removing many of Wollstonecraft's assertions in the first-person singular, making for a more conventional, objective, and academic style.[11]

From the beginning, it seems that Godwin was quick to criticize Wollstonecraft's writing style. He explains, for example, in the *Memoirs* that, prior to meeting her at Johnson's dinner party in 1791, he had dipped into her '*Answer to Burke*, and had been displeased, as literary men are apt to be, with a few offenses [*sic*] against grammar and other minute points of composition. I had therefore little curiosity to see Mrs Wollstonecraft' (*M*. 236). Five years later, when the two were courting, Wollstonecraft agreed to take lessons in grammar from her future husband: 'You are to give me a lesson this evening,' she reminds him in a letter of 15 September 1796 (*CL* 351). 'And, a word in your ear,' she adds flirtatiously, 'I shall not be very angry if you sweeten grammatical disquisitions after the Miltonic mode – Fancy, at this moment, has turned a conjunction into a kiss' (*CL* 351). Grammatical instruction apart, Wollstonecraft resisted Godwin's efforts to render her style more impersonal, to rob her writing of the assertive first-person singular, and reduce the vibrant individuality of her voice to a dull anonymous monotone. In the following letter, she defends herself against Godwin's wounding remark that her writing has 'a radical defect in it'.

> By what I have already written Johnson, I am sure, has been a gainer. And, for I would wish you to see my heart and mind just as it appears to myself, without drawing any veil of affected humility over it, though this whole letter is a proof of painful diffidence, I am compelled to think that there is some thing in my writings more valuable, than in the productions of some people on whom you bestow warm elogiums – I mean more mind – denominate it as you will – more of the observations of my own senses, more of the combining of my own imagination – the effusion of my own feelings and passions than the cold workings of the brain on the materials procured by the senses and imagination of other writers. (*CL* 345)

The warm reception given to *Letters from Sweden*, and, once the scandal surrounding Godwin's *Memoirs* abated, to the frank and painful 'Letters to Imlay', suggests that Wollstonecraft was correct to insist on the superior emotional force of (Romantic) self-expression over (Enlightenment) reason.

Alongside the essay 'On Poetry', Godwin included in the *Posthumous Works* a set of writings that he called 'Hints (chiefly designed to have been incorporated in the Second Part of the *Vindication of the Rights of Woman*)'. Comprising a series of thirty-two aphoristic sentences and short paragraphs, 'Hints' covers a range of subjects, including the status of women and female education. As Jump notes, however, the body of 'Hints' is concerned with ideas about the imagination, about poetry, and about the relation of reason to feeling, that are addressed in the essay 'On Poetry'. So close is the resemblance between the two texts on these subjects, that Jump urges us to view 'Hints', not as preparation for the second part of *Rights of Woman*, but as 'material intended for, but never incorporated into the essay "On Poetry", which shares many of their ideas'.[12] Those ideas, on the individuality of seeing and the genius of the poetic imagination, culminate in the penultimate 'Hint', which reinforces the view given in 'On Poetry' that true genius resides within the individual perceiving subject and is expressed by the ingenuity of his or her emotional response to the natural world:

> It is the individual manner of seeing and feeling, pourtrayed [*sic*] by a strong imagination in bold images that have struck the senses, which creates all the charms of poetry. A great reader is always quoting the description of another's emotions; a strong imagination delights to paint its own. A writer of genius makes us feel; an inferior author reason. (v. 276)

Notwithstanding her interest in intellectual questions to do with aesthetics and the poetic imagination, Wollstonecraft continued to address rather more basic questions concerning the education of children. Godwin published as an appendix to *The Wrongs of Woman* the 'first book of a series' of lessons which, Wollstonecraft announces in the heading to the text, 'I intended to have written for my unfortunate girl' (iv. 468). Godwin entitled the production 'Lessons', which he suggests in an editorial note in the *Posthumous Works* were probably 'written in a period of desperation, in the month of October, 1795' – the month of Wollstonecraft's second suicide attempt (iv. 468). The slim 'first book' of 'Lessons', the only one that Wollstonecraft completed, consists of elementary lessons on grammar and spelling together with advice on basic hygiene and safety. The form of the text is not dissimilar from contemporary books for very young children. The sentences are short and imperative, and are intended to teach a child parental obedience and correct behaviour, often through examples from the animal world. Lesson XII, for example, opens with the sentences: 'Look at those two dogs. The old one brings the ball to me in a moment; the young one does not know how. He must be taught' (iv. 473).

The second educational text to be included by Godwin in the *Posthumous Works* is also unfinished. 'Fragment of Letters on the Management of Infants' was intended by Wollstonecraft to form part of a series of seven letters on this subject. The 'Fragment' published by Godwin addresses the problem of infant mortality. In an effort to stem the high death rate of one in three, Wollstonecraft calls on mothers, especially those belonging to the middle class, to treat childcare as a profession to be learned, to approach it with a rational attitude.

In the two centuries since Wollstonecraft's death numerous biographies and scholarly studies have appeared. Godwin's book is the one that comes closest to the revolutionary spirit of her own work: just as Wollstonecraft's hallmark was to create new rules for old genres, so the *Memoirs* marks an innovation in the history of literary biography. Its psychological insight singled it out from the beginning as a truly original work. Not content with chronicling the events of Wollstonecraft's life, with unexpected frankness Godwin attempts to elucidate her philosophy and to show its impact on her work. He neither hides her imperfections nor plays down her genius. Unsurprisingly, his book has remained a staple resource of modern biographers. Notwithstanding that feat, nor discrediting the achievement of the many excellent biographies and articles that have since appeared, it is Virginia Woolf's short essay on Wollstonecraft, published in 1932, that is most in sympathy with her heroine. While many, including Godwin, have found themselves excusing, or at the very least explaining, her suicide attempts, her affairs, her suspicion of female sexuality, and her indulgence in it, Woolf writes with the understanding of one who had similarly struggled with the intractable contradictions of life; who refused to be cowed by convention and who preferred suicide to compromise. Wollstonecraft's life and work, writes Woolf, was a constant experiment, and it is a sign of her originality that so much of what she wrote and thought has now become commonplace:

> as we read her letters and listen to her arguments and consider her experiments, above all, that most fruitful experiment, her relation with Godwin, and realise the high-handed and hot-blooded manner in which she cut her way to the quick of life, one form of immortality is hers undoubtedly: she is alive and active, she argues and experiments, we hear her voice and trace her influence even now among the living.[13]

Notes

CHAPTER 1. INTRODUCTION: AN EXTRAORDINARY WOMAN

1. On Blake's admiration of Wollstonecraft, see William M. Gaunt, *Arrows of Desire: A Study of William Blake and his Romantic World* (London: Museum Press Ltd., 1956), 86–90. Gaunt suggests that Blake's poem 'Mary', the subject of which is a beautiful female outcast, invokes Wollstonecraft's abandonment by Imlay. Claire Tomalin adds that Coleridge's 'Kubla Khan' and Wordsworth's 'Ruth' also draw poetic sustenance from the story of Wollstonecraft's desertion by Imlay. See *LD* 239, 291 n.
2. Miriam Brody (ed.), *Vindication of the Rights of Woman* (1975; repr. Harmondsworth: Penguin, 1986), 55.
3. Virginia Woolf, 'Mary Wollstonecraft', *The Common Reader. Second Series* (1932; repr. London: The Hogarth Press, 1965), 156–63, 159.

CHAPTER 2. EARLY REBELLION

1. Wollstonecraft told Imlay, in a letter written in 1794, that she had 'always been half in love' with Rousseau (vi. 387). Locke's treatise *Some Thoughts Concerning Education* (1693) advocated the importance of teaching children by example rather than by abstract rules. Wollstonecraft shared this view and endorses Locke's 'system' in *Education of Daughters* (iv. 9).
2. In a letter to Everina, written in late autumn 1793, Wollstonecraft mentions Eliza's depression, adding that 'she seems to think she has been very ill used' (*CL* 80).
3. See Janet Todd, *Women's Friendship in Literature* (New York: Columbia University Press, 1980), 360. On Marie Antoinette's rumoured lesbianism, see Terry Castle, *The Apparitional Lesbian: Female Homosexuality and Modern Culture* (New York: Columbia

University Press, 1993), 107–49. Castle's claim, made in the *London Review of Books* (3 Aug. 1995), 3–6, that Austen's relationship with her sister Cassandra was unquestionably the most important emotional relationship of her life provoked a heated debate on the subject of Austen's sexuality in the 'Letters' page of the *LRB* that raged for four months.

4. Although Wollstonecraft was suspicious of the orthodox clergy, whom she viewed as corrupt and careerist, she believed in the Deity and subscribed to the religious doctrine that suffering on earth was necessary preparation for the afterlife. Gary Kelly observes that religious resignation played a continuing part in shaping her self-identity, offering compensation for her social alienation and inward conflict. Yet he also remarks that she increasingly placed more emphasis on the importance of critical thought to moral behaviour. See *RF* 37–8. Further details of Wollstonecraft's ethical and religious views can be found in Emma Rauschenbush-Clough, *A Study of Mary Wollstonecraft and the Rights of Woman* (London: Longmans, Green & Co., 1898), 46–66. See also Mary Wilson Carpenter, 'Sibylline Apocalyptics: Mary Wollstonecraft's *Vindication of the Rights of Woman* and Job's Mother's Womb', *Literature and History*, 12/2 (1986), 215–28. Carpenter offers a persuasive interpretation of *Rights of Woman* as a feminist reworking of biblical prophecy. See also Barbara Taylor, 'For the Love of God: Religion and the Erotic Imagination in Wollstonecraft's Feminism', in Eileen Janes Yeo (ed. *Mary Wollstonecraft and 200 Years of Feminisms* (London and New York: Rivers Oram Press, 1997), 15–35.

5. On Hewlett's introduction of Wollstonecraft to her publisher Johnson, see *CL* 94 n. 2. Her meeting with Dr Johnson, whom she visited in the last year of his life, is recorded in *LD* 50–1.

6. The statement provides another example of Wollstonecraft's religious conviction that our earthly life is a 'probationary' period in which we suffer in preparation for our exaltation to happier state in death.

7. Clarissa and Sophie are the idealized heroines of Samuel Richardson's novel *Clarissa* (1747–8), and of Rousseau's fiction *Émile* (1762), respectively.

8. In a letter to Everina, dated 24 Mar. 1787, Wollstonecraft wrote: 'I am now reading Rousseau's Emile, and love his paradoxes. He chuses [*sic*] a *common* capacity to educate – and gives as a reason, that a genius will educate itself' (*CL* 145).

9. Fanny Blood, on whom Ann is modelled, came from an impoverished Irish family to whom Wollstonecraft frequently offered aid. She used the money she received from the publication

of *Education of Daughters*, for example, to fund the passage of Fanny's parents to their native country.

10. *English Review*, 16 (1790), 465; *Monthly Review*, NS 2 (1790), 352–3. Cited in Mary Wollstonecraft, *Mary. A Fiction*, ed. and intro. Caroline Franklin (London: Routledge/Thoemmes Press, 1995), p. xvi.

11. See Todd, *Women's Friendship in Literature*, 192–208.

12. *Mary*, ed. Franklin, p. v.

CHAPTER 3. PROFESSIONAL WORKS

1. See Roy Porter, *English Society in the Eighteenth Century* (1982; repr. Harmondsworth: Penguin, 1988), 295–6.

2. Heather Glen, *Vision and Disenchantment: Blake's* Songs & *Wordsworth's* Lyrical Ballads (Cambridge: Cambridge University Press, 1983), 9.

3. The scandals surrounding the Kingsborough family are recorded in *LD* 87, 294–6.

4. On the tricky issue of establishing her contributions to the *Analytical Review* which were signed with various initials, see Sally N. Stewart, 'Mary Wollstonecraft's Contributions to the *Analytical Review*', *Essays in English Literature*, 11 (1984), 187–99.

5. There remains a question mark, however, over why Wollstonecraft did not acknowledge *The Female Reader* as her own work. See Stewart, 'Mary Wollstoncraft's Contributions'.

6. Charles Kegan Paul, *William Godwin: His Friends and Contemporaries* (London: Henry S. King & Co., 1876), 193.

CHAPTER 4. REVOLUTIONARY PROTEST

1. This is the figure given by Henry Collins in the introduction to his edition of Paine's *Rights of Men* (Harmondsworth: Penguin, 1969; repr. 1983), 36.

2. Michèle Cohen, *Fashioning Masculinity: National Identity and Language in the Eighteenth Century* (London and New York: Routledge, 1996), 9.

3. Cited in Edmund Burke, *Reflections on the Revolution in France*, ed. and intro. Connor Cruise O'Brien (1968, repr. Harmondsworth: Penguin, 1986), 24.

4. Ibid. 119.

5. Cora Kaplan, 'Wild Nights: Pleasure/Sexuality/Feminism', *Sea Changes: Culture and Feminism* (London: Verso, 1986), 31–56, at 39.

6. Barbara Taylor, 'Mary Wollstonecraft and the Wild Wish of Early Feminism', *History Workshop Journal*, 33 (1992), 197–219, at 217.
7. Ibid. 217.
8. See e.g. Darian Leader's psychoanalytic exploration of male and female attitudes to sex and romance, *Why Do Women Write More Letters than they Post?* (London: Faber, 1996), which has been translated into fourteen languages. For further examples of male guides to relationships and sexuality, see Robert Bly, *Iron John: A Book about Men* (London: Element, 1994); Daniel Goleman, *Emotional Intelligence: Why It Can Matter more than IQ* (London: Bloomsbury, 1996).
9. Critics have disagreed over the degree to which *Wrongs of Woman* can be said to subvert the structure of traditional romantic fiction. Mary Poovey argues that, while Wollstonecraft sets out to question 'romantic expectations', her fictions get caught up in the very ideology they aim to critique. See Poovey, *The Proper Lady and the Woman Writer: Ideology as Style in the Works of Mary Wollstoncraft , Mary Shelley, and Jane Austen* (Chicago: University of Chicago Press, 1984), 98. Vivien Jones, however, reads *Wrongs of Woman* as an 'alternative romance' that exposes women's sexual exploitation in patriarchy. See Jones, ' "The Tyranny of the Passions": Feminism and Heterosexuality in the Fiction of Wollstonecraft and Hays', in Sally Ledger, Josephine McDonagh, and Jane Spencer (eds.), *Political Gender: Texts and Contexts* (London: Harvester, 1994), 173–88.
10. See Elaine Jordan, 'Criminal Conversation: On Mary Wollstonecraft's *The Wrongs of Woman*', *Women's Writing*, 4/2 (1997), 221–34.
11. Ibid. 224.

CHAPTER 5.   ROMANTIC VENTURES

1. Roscoe's ballad, 'The Life, Death and Wonderful Atchievements of Edmund Burke', is cited in *LD* 127. The third stanza reads as follows:

> An lo! an Amazon stept out,
>   One WOLLSTONECRAFT her name,
> Resolv'd to stop his mad career,
>   Whatever chance became.

2. The portraits make an interesting coda to Wollstonecraft's professional and private life. The first of Opie's portraits of her, which hangs in the Tate Gallery and was painted *c.*1791–2, between the publication of her two *Vindications*, shows her in

formal dress, her hair powdered grey. She is seated at her desk with an open book in her hand, from which she looks up at the spectator. For further discussion of this portrait, which is reproduced as the frontispiece to this study, see Mary Peter, 'A Portrait of Mary Wollstonecraft Godwin in the Tate Gallery', *Keats–Shelley Memorial Bulletin*, 14 (1963), 1–3. The second of Opie's portraits, painted in 1797, gives a far more feminine picture of Wollstonecraft, corresponding to the shift in the public perception of her that occurred after the publication of *Letters from Sweden*, which I discuss in Chapter 6. In this portrait, Wollstonecraft's long auburn hair is loosely tied at the nape of her neck and her gaze is softer, more expressive, and less challenging than in the earlier painting. She is dressed in a revealing garment, made of flimsy material, that falls open at the neck. The portrait is reproduced on the cover of this study. Two 'prettified' versions of this portrait, which adapt Wollstonecraft's image to bring it close to conventional standards of beauty are reproduced in *LD*, plates 19 and 21.

3. The portrait commissioned by Roscoe was painted by an unknown artist in 1791, when Wollstonecraft was 32. It is the earliest known portrait of her, and depicts her as a sober governess and intellectual. Her sensible dress and powdered hair make her appear far older than her years. The portrait is reproduced in *LD*, plate 1.

4. Ralph Wardle notes that *Défense des droits des femmes*, a French translation of *Rights of Woman*, was published at Paris and Lyons in 1792. See *CL* 214 n. 3.

5. Christian Gotthilf Salzmann, who is mentioned in Chapter 3, translated *Rights of Woman* into German in 1793–4. An edition was published in Boston, USA, in 1792, followed by two editions printed in Philadelphia, both in 1794. An Irish edition was printed in Dublin in 1793.

6. Williams's *Letters Written in France* (1790) were reviewed in the *Analytical Review* in December 1790. The reviewer, who may have been Wollstonecraft, describes them as 'truly feminine'. See vii. 322.

7. Wollstonecraft's association with the Girondins, and with Madame Roland in particular, is discussed in detail in Chapter 11 of *LD* 156–82. See especially 174–7.

8. On Williams's elopement with Stone, see *LD* 164.

9. Extracts from Imlay's books are reproduced and discussed in *PS* 226–46. A modern reprint of *The Emigrants* appeared in 1998, edited by W. M. Verhoeven and Amanda Gilroy, and published in London by Penguin.

10. Jane Rendall, '"The grand causes which combine to carry

mankind forward": Wollstonecraft, history and revolution', *Women's Writing*, 4/2 (1997), 155–72, 156–7.

11. Cited in Harriet Devine Jump, '"The Cool Eye of Observation": Mary Wollstoncraft and the French Revolution', in Kelvin Everest (ed.), *Revolution in Writing: British Literary Responses to the French Revolution* (Milton Keynes: Open University Press, 1991), 101–19, at 101.

12. *British Critic* (July 1795), 29–36, at 35.

13. The passage is reproduced as it appears in the *British Critic* (July 1795), 35.

14. Rendall, '"The grand causes"', 167.

15. Richard Cobb, 'Radicalism and Wreckage', *The Times Literary Supplement* (6 Sept. 1974), 941–4, at 943.

CHAPTER 6.   FINAL DESTINATIONS

1. Shelley, in his Dedication to Mary Shelley of 'The Revolt of Islam' (1817), wrote of Wollstonecraft:

   > They say that thou were lovely from thy birth,
   > Of glorious parents, thou aspiring child;
   > I wonder not – for one then left this earth
   > Whose life was like a setting planet mild,
   > Which clothed thee in the radiance undefiled
   > Of its departing glory; still her fame
   > Shines on thee, through the tempests dark and wild
   > Which shake these latter days; and thou canst claim
   > The shelter, from thy Sire, of an immortal name.
   >
   > (Cited in *PS*, pp. xxxiv–xxxv)

2. Southey wrote to his friend Joseph Cottle: 'Have you met with Mary Wollstonecraft's [travel book]? She has made me in love with a cold climate, and frost and snow, with a northern moonlight' (cited in *M.* 17). Southey also wrote two admiring poems about Wollstonecraft (see PS, pp. xxx–xxxi). Thomas Holcroft was so fascinated by her that he wished to have her corpse opened in the supposition that an autopsy would reveal the source of her passionate being. On this, see Anya Taylor, 'Coleridge, Wollstonecraft, and the Rights of Woman', in Tim Fulford and Morton D. Paley (eds.), *Coleridge's Visionary Languages* (Cambridge: D. S. Brewer, 1993), 83–98.

3. *British Critic*, vol. 7 (Jan.–June 1796), 602–10, at 602.

4. Ibid. 607.

5. See Claire Tomalin, *Jane Austen: A Life* (Harmondsworth: Viking

1997), 158–9.

6. For a detailed account of Wollstonecraft's death, which analyses its 'ideological ironies' as well as its implications for feminism, see Vivien Jones, 'The Death of Mary Wollstonecraft', *British Journal for Eighteenth-Century Studies*, 40/2 (Autumn 1997), 187–95.

7. Margaret Tims, *Mary Wollstonecraft: A Social Pioneer* (London: Millington Books Ltd, 1976), 345.

8. *Monthly Magazine*, 3 (Apr. 1797), 279–89.

9. Harriet Devine Jump, '"A Kind of Witchcraft": Mary Wollstonecraft and the Poetic Imagination', *Women's Writing*, 4/2 (1997), 235–45, at 235–6.

10. Ibid. 238.

11. Ibid. 241.

12. Ibid. 240.

13. Virginia Woolf, 'Mary Wollstonecraft', *The Common Reader, Second Series* (1932; repr. London: The Hogarth Press, 1965), 163.

Select Bibliography

WORKS BY MARY WOLLSTONECRAFT

The most complete collection of Wollstonecraft's writing is *The Works of Mary Wollstonecraft*, ed. Janet Todd and Marilyn Butler (7 vols.; London: Pickering & Chatto, 1989). This edition contains almost everything known to be written by Wollstonecraft, including her translations, reviews, posthumous writings, and some of her letters. Dates given below are to the first publication of the works. Roman numerals placed within square brackets refer to the relevant volume number of *The Works of Mary Wollstonecraft*.

Books

Thoughts on the Education of Daughters: with Reflections on Female Conduct, in the More Important Duties of Life (London: Joseph Johnson, 1787), [iv].

Mary. A Fiction (London: Joseph Johnson, 1788) [i].

Original Stories from Real Life: with Conversations Calculated to Regulate the Affections and Form the Mind to Truth and Goodness (London: Joseph Johnson, 1788) [iv].

The Female Reader; or, Miscellaneous Pieces, in Prose and Verse; Selected from the Best Writers, and Disposed under Proper Heads: for the Improvement of Young Women (London: Joseph Johnson, 1789) [iv].

A Vindication of the Rights of Men, in a Letter to the Right Honourable Edmund Burke (London: Joseph Johnson, 1790) [v].

Vindication of the Rights of Woman: with Strictures on Political and Moral Subjects (London: Joseph Johnson, 1792) [v].

An Historical and Moral View of the Origin and Progress of the French Revolution; and the Effect it has produced in Europe (London: Joseph Johnson, 1794) [vi].

Letters Written During a Short Residence in Sweden, Norway and Denmark (London: Joseph Johnson, 1796) [vi].

Translations and Reviews

Of the Importance of Religious Opinions. Translated from the French of Mr. Necker (London: Joseph Johnson, 1788) [iii].

Young Grandison. A Series of Letters from Young Persons to their Friends. Translated from the Dutch of Madame de Cambon. With Alterations and Improvements (2 vols.; London: Joseph Johnson, 1790) [ii].

Elements of Morality, for the Use of Children; with an Introductory Address to Parents. Translated from the German of Rev. C. G. Salzmann (2 vols.; London: Joseph Johnson, 1790) [ii].

Contributions to the *Analytical Review* 1788–97 [vii].

Posthumous Works

The following works were first published in William Godwin (ed.), *Posthumous Works of the Author of A Vindication of the Rights of Woman in Four Volumes* (London: Joseph Johnson, 1798).

The Wrongs of Woman: or, Maria. A Fragment [i].

'Extract of the Cave of Fancy. A Tale' [i].

'Hints. (Chiefly designed to have been incorporated in the Second Part of the Vindication of the Rights of Woman)' [v].

'Letters to Imlay' [vi].

'Letter Introductory to a Series of Letters on the Present Character of the French Nation' [vi].

'Letters to Mr. Johnson, Bookseller in St Paul's Church-Yard' [vi].

'Fragment of Letters on the Management of Infants' [iv].

'Lessons' [iv].

'On Poetry, and Our Relish for the Beauties of Nature', first published in the *Monthly Magazine* (Apr. 1797), 279–82 [vii].

Collections of Letters

The Love Letters of Mary Wollstonecraft to Gilbert Imlay, with a Prefatory Memoir by Roger Ingpen (London: Hutchinson & Co., 1908).

Memoirs of Mary Wollstonecraft Written by William Godwin. Edited with a Preface and a Supplement and a Bibliographical Note, ed. William Clark Durant (London: Constable & Co., Ltd., 1927).

Four New Letters of Mary Wollstonecraft and Helen Maria Williams, ed. Benjamin P. Kurtz and Carrie C. Autrey (Berkeley and Los Angeles: University of California Press, 1937).

Shelley and his Circle: 1773–1822, ed. Kenneth Neill Cameron (Cambridge, Mass.: Harvard University Press, 1961).

Godwin and Mary: Letters, ed. Ralph M. Wardle (Lawrence, Kan.: University of Kansas Press, 1966; London: Constable, 1967).

Collected Letters of Mary Wollstonecraft, ed. Ralph M. Wardle (Ithaca and London: Cornell University Press, 1979).

Separate Editions of Works

Vindication of the Rights of Woman, ed. Miriam Brody (1975; repr. Harmondsworth: Penguin, 1986).

A Vindication of the Rights of Men with A Vindication of the Rights of Woman and Hints, ed. Sylvana Tomaselli (Cambridge: Cambridge University Press, 1995).

Political Writings, ed. Janet Todd (Oxford: Oxford University Press, 1994). This edition includes *A Vindication of the Rights of Men*, *Vindication of the Rights of Woman*, and an abridged version of *An Historical and Moral View of the Origin and Progress of the French Revolution*.

Mary and the Wrongs of Woman, ed. James Kinsley and Gary Kelly (Oxford: Oxford University Press, 1980). This edition includes *Mary. A Fiction* and *The Wrongs of Woman: or, Maria*.

A Short Residence in Sweden and Memoirs of the Author of 'The Rights of Woman', ed. Richard Holmes (Harmondsworth: Penguin, 1987). This edition includes *Letters Written During a Short Residence in Sweden, Norway and Denmark* and Godwin's *Memoirs*.

A Wollstonecraft Anthology, ed. Janet Todd (Bloomington and Indianapolis: Indiana University Press, 1977). Contains a selection of Wollstonecraft's less well-known works.

BIBLIOGRAPHY

For an extensive annotated bibliography, including nineteenth- and early twentieth-century biographies and essays, see Janet Todd, *Mary Wollstonecraft: An Annotated Bibliography* (New York and London: Garland Publishing Inc., 1976).

BIOGRAPHY

There are numerous excellent critical biographies of Wollstonecraft. Many of them appeared in the 1970s and are reviewed in Janet Todd's article, 'The Biographies of Mary Wollstonecraft', *Signs*, 1 (1976), 721–34.

Flexner, Eleanor, *Mary Wollstonecraft: A Biography* (New York: Coward, 1972). Scholarly history of the life and works. Contains an analytical bibliography.

George, Margaret, *One Woman's 'Situation': A Biography* (Urbana, Ill.: University of Illinois Press, 1970). Psychoanalytical biography, written from the perspective of a sympathetic female reader. George maintains that scholars have failed to empathize with Wollstonecraft's 'situation'.

Godwin, William, *Memoirs of the Author of A Vindication of the Rights of Woman* (London: Joseph Johnson, 1798). Pioneering psychobiography that shocked contemporary readers with its revolutionary frankness. Invaluable source of information about Wollstonecraft's personality, her relationships, and her philosophy.

Rauschenbush-Clough, Emma, *A Study of Mary Wollstonecraft and the Rights of Woman* (London: Longmans, Green & Co., 1898). Early scholarly attempt to present Wollstonecraft as a serious thinker. Includes a helpful chapter on her religious and ethical views.

St Clair, William, *The Godwins and the Shelleys: The Biography of A Family* (New York and London: W. W. Norton & Company, 1989). Dynamic social and political history of the Wollstonecraft and Godwin dynasty, as well as a literary history of the Romantic age.

Tims, Margaret, *Mary Wollstonecraft: A Social Pioneer* (London: Millington Books Ltd, 1976). Presents the life of a woman who has 'thinking powers', as Wollstonecraft described her own heroine in *Mary. A Fiction*.

Tomalin, Claire, *The Life and Death of Mary Wollstonecraft* (rev. edn., Harmondsworth: Penguin, 1992). First published in 1974, this highly readable and well-researched book remains the best modern biography of Wollstonecraft. Provides a rich and sympathetic portrait of her character, and contains useful information on the intellectual context of her work.

Wardle, Ralph M., *Mary Wollstonecraft: A Critical Biography* (Lawrence, Kan.: University of Kansas Press, 1951). Scholarly analysis which put Wollstonecraft's writings on the academic map after decades of neglect. Wardle is accused of lacking in empathy for Wollstonecraft as woman by Margaret George, in *One Woman's 'Situation'*.

CRITICAL WORKS

For a writer of the range and diversity of Wollstonecraft there are surprisingly few recent monographs on her work. Exclusive studies, other than biographies, include:

Jump, Harriet Devine, *Mary Wollstonecraft: Writer* (Hemel Hempstead: Harvester Wheatsheaf, 1994). A concise introduction to the whole body of Wollstonecraft's work. Includes new material on Wollstonecraft's links with Burke and the later Romantic poets.

Kelly, Gary, *Revolutionary Feminism: The Mind and Career of Mary Wollstonecraft* (London: Macmillan, 1992). Essential reading: detailed examination of all Wollstonecraft's writings. Situates her feminism in the context of her life and in relation to the intellectual debates sparked in Britain by the French Revolution. Especially good on the experimental quality of her writing.

Lorch, Jennifer, *Mary Wollstonecraft: The Making of a Radical Feminist* (Providence, RI: Berg, 1990). Charts the growth of Wollstonecraft's feminist thought; argues that *Wrongs of Woman* is more relevant to the concerns of late twentieth-century feminism than *Rights of Woman*.

Sapiro, Virginia, *Vindication of Political Virtue: The Political Theory of Mary Wollstonecraft* (Chicago and London: Chicago University Press, 1992). Thematic consideration of all Wollstonecraft's writings as the work of a committed political theorist.

STUDIES

What follows is a select bibliography of essays published in books and scholarly journals, as well as books of a more general nature that include some discussion of Wollstonecraft's work or provide information relevant to her social and intellectual background.

Alexander, Meena, *Women in Romanticism* (London: Macmillan, 1989). Examines Wollstonecraft's novels, and educational and political works, linking them through the theme of maternity to the Romantic writings of Dorothy Wordsworth and Mary Shelley.

Brody, Miriam (ed. and intro.), *Vindication of the Rights of Woman* (1975; repr. Harmondsworth: Penguin, 1986). Includes a comprehensive introduction that examines the historical specificity of Wollstonecraft's text and explores its influence on the development of modern feminism.

Burdett, Carolyn, 'A Difficult Vindication: Olive Schreiner's Wollstonecraft Introduction', *History Workshop Journal*, 37 (1994), 177–93. Insightful essay on the problems Schreiner faced in preparing her (unfinished) introduction to *Rights of Woman*.

Butler, Marilyn (ed. and intro.), *Burke, Paine, Godwin, and the Revolution Controversy* (Cambridge: Cambridge University Press, 1984). Contains a perspicacious introduction to excerpts from the writings of British pro-Revolutionaries, including Wollstonecraft.

Carpenter, Mary Wilson, 'Sibylline Apocalyptics: Mary Wollstonecraft's *Vindication of the Rights of Woman* and Job's Mother's Womb', *Literature and History*, 12/2 (1986), 215–28. Innovative study of Wollstonecraft's antagonistic reading of biblical prophecy.

Castle, Terry, *The Apparitional Lesbian: Female Homosexuality and Modern Culture* (New York: Columbia University Press, 1993). Cultural history of lesbian heroines, including the eighteenth-century icon Marie Antoinette.

—— *The Female Thermometer: Eighteenth-Century Culture and the Invention of the Uncanny* (New York and Oxford: Oxford University Press, 1995). Castle's exploration of the subversive role of Gothic fiction, sexual masquerade, and sexual impersonation in the 'age of reason' provides a fascinating context for understanding Wollstonecraft's suspicion of erotic behaviour.

Everest, Kelvin (ed.), *Revolution in Writing: British Literary Responses to the French Revolution* (Milton Keynes: Open University Press, 1991). Important collection of essays on Wollstonecraft's, Paine's, and Burke's responses to the French Revolution.

Ferguson, Frances, 'Wollstonecraft our Contemporary', in Linda Kauffman (ed.), *Gender and Theory: Dialogues on Feminist Criticism* (Oxford: Basil Blackwell, 1989), 51–62. Takes modern critics to task for allowing their interests to overshadow the historical specificity of *Rights of Woman*.

Ferguson, Moira, *Colonialism and Gender from Mary Wollstonecraft to Jamaica Kincaid: East Caribbean Relations* (New York: Columbia University Press, 1993). Contains a chapter on Wollstonecraft and slavery.

Gaunt, William M., *Arrows of Desire: A Study of William Blake and his Romantic World* (London: Museum Press Ltd., 1956). Useful corrective to the recent view of Wollstonecraft as a sexual puritan. Introduces the notion that in her struggle against contemporary sexual mores, particularly her rejection of conventional marriage, Wollstonecraft represented Blake's 'Ideal Woman'.

Gubar, Susan, 'Feminist Misogyny: Mary Wollstonecraft and the Paradox of "It Takes One to Know One"', in Diane Elam and Robyn Wiegman (eds.), *Feminism Beside Itself* (New York and London: Routledge, 1995), 133–54. Suggestive but highly debatable essay that finds evidence of 'feminist misogyny' in Wollstonecraft's analysis of femininity.

Guest, Harriet, 'The dream of a common language: Hannah More and Mary Wollstonecraft', *Textual Practice*, 9/2 (1995), 303–23. Illuminating analysis of the similarities in the arguments of *Rights of Woman* and the apparently more conservative *Strictures on the Modern System of Female Education* (1799) by Hannah More.

Hill, Bridget, 'The Links between Mary Wollstonecraft and Catherine Macaulay: New Evidence', *Women's History Review*, 4/2 (1995), 177–92. Reprints an epistolary exchange between the authors, occasioned by the publication of Burke's *Reflections on the Revolution in France*, and analyses the similarities in their views on democracy, equality, and women's rights.

Holmes, Richard (ed. and intro.), *A Short Residence in Sweden, Norway and Denmark and Memoirs of the Author of The Rights of Woman* (Harmondsworth: Penguin, 1987). Holmes's elegant introduction is full of brilliant insights into Wollstonecraft's relationships with Imlay and Godwin, as well as her contribution to literary Romanticism.

Jacobus, Mary, 'The Difference of View', *Women Writing and Writing about Women* (London: Croom Helm, 1979), 10–21. Feminist analysis of *Wrongs of Woman* as an illustration of women writers' troubled relationship to the language of sentiment and romance.

Jones, Vivien, ' "The Tyranny of the Passions": Feminism and Heterosexuality in the Fiction of Wollstonecraft and Hays', in Sally Ledger, Josephine McDonagh, and Jane Spencer (eds.), *Political Gender: Texts and Contexts* (London: Harvester, 1994), 173–88. Reads *Wrongs of Woman* and Mary Hay's novel *Memoirs of Emma Courtney* (1796) as fictions that rewrite the inherited form of eighteenth-century sentimental romance from a feminist perspective.

—— (ed. and intro.), *Women in the Eighteenth Century: Constructions of Femininity* (London and New York: Routledge, 1990). Includes an informative introductory essay to excerpts from eighteenth-century conduct books, educational works, feminist treatises, reviews, and essays. Invaluable for setting Wollstonecraft's work in its contemporary context.

Jordan, Elaine, 'Criminal Conversation: On Mary Wollstonecraft's *The Wrongs of Woman*', *Women's Writing*, 4/2 (1997), 221–34. Examines the contemporary legal discourses that inform *Wrongs of Woman*.

Jump, Harriet Devine, ' "A Kind of Witchcraft": Mary Wollstonecraft and the Poetic Imagination', *Women's Writing*, 4/2 (1997), 235–45. Reads the essay 'On Poetry' as evidence of Wollstonecraft's increasing emphasis on the importance of the poetic imagination.

—— ' "The Cool Eye of Observation": Mary Wollstonecraft and the French Revolution', in Kelvin Everest (ed.), *Revolution in Writing: British Literary Responses to the French Revolution* (Milton Keynes: Open University Press, 1991), 101–19. A reading of Wollstonecraft's *An Historical and Moral View of the Origin and Progress of the French Revolution*, which argues that the events in France in the early 1790s caused Wollstonecraft to question her earlier theoretical position on the consequences of Revolution.

Kaplan, Cora, *Sea Changes: Culture and Feminism* (London: Verso, 1986). Contains Kaplan's immensely influential studies of the troubled place of female sexuality in Wollstonecraft's feminism. See, 'Wild Nights: Pleasure/Sexuality/Feminism', 31–56, which examines Wollstonecraft's negative stance on female sexual pleasure in *Rights of*

Woman; and 'Pandora's Box: Subjectivity, Class and Sexuality in Socialist Feminist Criticism', 147–76.

Nussbaum, Felicity A., *Torrid Zones: Maternity, Sexuality, and Empire in Eighteenth-Century English Narratives* (Baltimore and London: The Johns Hopkins University Press, 1995). Postcolonial analysis that implicates *Rights of Woman* in the imperialist assumptions of European feminism.

Poovey, Mary, *The Proper Lady and the Woman Writer: Ideology as Style in the Works of Mary Wollstonecraft, Mary Shelley, and Jane Austen* (Chicago: Chicago University Press, 1984). Indispensable analysis of Wollstonecraft's ambivalent relation to romance and sexuality, as particularly evident in her novels and in *Rights of Woman*.

Rendall, Jane, *The Origins of Modern Feminism: Women in Britain. France and the United States 1780–1860* (London: Macmillan, 1985). Comprehensive study of the subject.

—— ' "The grand causes which combine to carry mankind forward": Wollstonecraft, History and Revolution', *Women's Writing* 4/2 (1997), 155–72. Places Wollstonecraft's *An Historical and Moral View of the Origin and Progress of the French Revolution* in the context of contemporary historical writing, particularly that of the Scottish Enlightenment.

Spencer, Jane, *The Rise of the Woman Novelist: From Aphra Behn to Jane Austen* (Oxford: Basil Blackwell, 1986). Charts the tradition of the woman's novel in the eighteenth century. Places *Wrongs of Woman* in the context of radicalism and the novel of seduction.

Stewart, Sally N., 'Mary Wollstonecraft's Contributions to the *Analytical Review*', *Essays in English Literature*, 11 (1984), 187–99. Identifies some of Wollstonecraft's contributions to *Analytical Review*.

Taylor, Barbara, *Eve and the New Jerusalem: Socialism and Feminism in the Nineteenth Century* (London: Virago, 1983). Rigorous and invigorating history of women in radical nineteenth-century thought. Locates Wollstonecraft's feminism as a precursor of Owenite and other forms of nineteenth-century political utopianism.

—— 'Mary Wollstonecraft and the Wild Wish of Early Feminism', *History Workshop Journal*, 33 (1992), 197–219. Makes a persuasive case for interpreting Wollstonecraft's suspicion towards feminine sexuality in *Rights of Woman* as the inevitable consequence of her 'wild wish' to see the sexual distinction in society abolished.

—— 'For the Love of God: Religion and the Erotic Imagination in Wollstonecraft's Feminism', in Eileen Janes Yeo (ed.), *Mary Wollstonecraft and 200 Years of Feminisms* (London and New York: Rivers Oram Press, 1997), 15–35. Contains an extended analysis of the religious dimension of her thought.

Todd, Janet, *Women's Friendship in Literature* (New York: Columbia University Press, 1980). Sheds historical light on the vogue for intense female friendships in eighteenth-century literature and life. Includes biographical information on Wollstonecraft's relationship with Fanny Blood, as well as an astute reading of her novel, *The Wrongs of Woman: or, Maria*.

—— and Roberts, Marie-Mulvey (eds.), *Women's Writing*, Special Number: Mary Wollstonecraft: A Bicentennial, 4/2 (1997). Exciting collection of recent essays covering Wollstonecraft's response to the French Revolution, her relationship with Imlay, her theory of the poetic imagination, and her fictional writings.

Tomaselli, Sylvana (ed. and intro.), *A Vindication of the Rights of Men with A Vindication of the Rights of Woman and Hints* (Cambridge: Cambridge University Press, 1995). Includes a good historical introduction to the texts together with an informative and reliable bibliographical note.

—— 'The Enlightenment Debate on Women', *History Workshop Journal*, 20 (1988), 101–24. Examines in depth the position of women in eighteenth-century thought.

Wang, Orrin N. C., *Fantastic Modernity: Dialectical Readings in Romanticism and Theory* (Baltimore and London: The Johns Hopkins University Press, 1996). Includes an elaborate theoretical reading of *Rights of Woman* as a work that proleptically deconstructs the conventional categories of gender and Romanticism.

Woolf, Virginia, 'Mary Wollstonecraft', *The Common Reader. Second Series* (1932; repr. London: The Hogarth Press, 1965), 156–9. Stylish, sympathetic, and psychologically credible analysis of Wollstonecraft that celebrates her work and her life as a constant experiment.

Yeo, Eileen Janes (ed.), *Mary Wollstonecraft and 200 Years of Feminisms* (London and New York: Rivers Oram Press, 1997). Anthology of essays on Wollstonecraft's feminism arising from an international conference held at the University of Sussex in 1992. Has contributions from feminist historians, literary scholars, cultural critics, and political philosophers, many of whom are also activists.

Zonana, Joyce, 'The Sultan and the Slave: Feminist Orientalism and the Structure of *Jane Eyre*', *Signs*, 18/3 (1993), 592–617. Situates Wollstonecraft illuminatingly in a line of 'feminist orientalism' from Montesquieu's *Persian Letters* to Brontë's novel.

Index

Recent and
Forthcoming Titles
in the
New Series of

WRITERS AND
THEIR WORK

WRITERS AND THEIR WORK
RECENT & FORTHCOMING TITLES

Title	Author
Peter Ackroyd	*Susana Onega*
Kingsley Amis	*Richard Bradford*
As You Like It	*Penny Gay*
W.H. Auden	*Stan Smith*
Alan Ayckbourn	*Michael Holt*
J.G. Ballard	*Michel Delville*
Aphra Behn	*Sue Wiseman*
Edward Bond	*Michael Mangan*
Anne Brontë	*Betty Jay*
Emily Brontë	*Stevie Davies*
A.S. Byatt	*Richard Todd*
Caroline Drama	*Julie Sanders*
Angela Carter	*Lorna Sage*
Geoffrey Chaucer	*Steve Ellis*
Children's Literature	*Kimberley Reynolds*
Caryl Churchill	*Elaine Aston*
John Clare	*John Lucas*
S.T. Coleridge	*Stephen Bygrave*
Joseph Conrad	*Cedric Watts*
Crime Fiction	*Martin Priestman*
John Donne	*Stevie Davis*
Carol Ann Duffy	*Deryn Rees Jones*
George Eliot	*Josephine McDonagh*
English Translators of Homer	*Simeon Underwood*
Henry Fielding	*Jenny Uglow*
E.M. Forster	*Nicholas Royle*
Elizabeth Gaskell	*Kate Flint*
William Golding	*Kevin McCarron*
Graham Greene	*Peter Mudford*
Hamlet	*Ann Thompson & Neil Taylor*
Thomas Hardy	*Peter Widdowson*
David Hare	*Jeremy Ridgman*
Tony Harrison	*Joe Kelleher*
William Hazlitt	*J. B. Priestley; R. L. Brett* *(intro. by Michael Foot)*
Seamus Heaney	*Andrew Murphy*
George Herbert	*T.S. Eliot (intro. by Peter Porter)*
Henrik Ibsen	*Sally Ledger*
Henry James – The Later Writing	*Barbara Hardy*
James Joyce	*Steven Connor*
Julius Caesar	*Mary Hamer*
Franz Kafka	*Michael Wood*
King Lear	*Terence Hawkes*
Philip Larkin	*Laurence Lerner*
D.H. Lawrence	*Linda Ruth Williams*
Doris Lessing	*Elizabeth Maslen*
C.S. Lewis	*William Gray*
David Lodge	*Bernard Bergonzi*
Christopher Marlowe	*Thomas Healy*
Andrew Marvell	*Annabel Patterson*
Ian McEwan	*Kiernan Ryan*
Measure for Measure	*Kate Chedgzoy*
A Midsummer Night's Dream	*Helen Hackett*
Vladimir Nabokov	*Neil Cornwell*
V. S. Naipaul	*Suman Gupta*
Old English Verse	*Graham Holderness*
Walter Pater	*Laurel Brake*
Brian Patten	*Linda Cookson*

RECENT & FORTHCOMING TITLES

TITLES IN PREPARATION

Title	Author
Chinua Achebe	*Yousef Nahem*
Antony and Cleopatra	*Ken Parker*
Jane Austen	*Meenakshi Mukherjee*
Pat Barker	*Sharon Monteith*
Samuel Beckett	*Keir Elam*
John Betjeman	*Dennis Brown*
William Blake	*John Beer*
Elizabeth Bowen	*Maud Ellmann*
Charlotte Brontë	*Sally Shuttleworth*
Lord Byron	*Drummond Bone*
Daniel Defoe	*Jim Rigney*
Charles Dickens	*Rod Mengham*
Early Modern Sonneteers	*Michael Spiller*
T.S. Eliot	*Colin MacCabe*
Brian Friel	*Geraldine Higgins*
The *Gawain* Poetry	*John Burrow*
The Georgian Poets	*Rennie Parker*
Henry IV	*Peter Bogdanov*
Henry V	*Robert Shaughnessy*
Geoffrey Hill	*Andrew Roberts*
Christopher Isherwood	*Stephen Wade*
Kazuo Ishiguro	*Cynthia Wong*
Ben Jonson	*Anthony Johnson*
John Keats	*Kelvin Everest*
Charles and Mary Lamb	*Michael Baron*
Langland: *Piers Plowman*	*Claire Marshall*
Language Poetry	*Alison Mark*
Macbeth	*Kate McCluskie*
Katherine Mansfield	*Helen Haywood*
Harold Pinter	*Mark Batty*
Alexander Pope	*Pat Rogers*
Dennis Potter	*Derek Paget*
Religious Poets of the 17th Century	*Helen Wilcox*
Revenge Tragedy	*Janet Clare*
Richard III	*Edward Burns*
Siegfried Sassoon	*Jenny Hartley*
Mary Shelley	*Catherine Sharrock*
Stevie Smith	*Alison Light*
Muriel Spark	*Brian Cheyette*
Gertrude Stein	*Nicola Shaughnessy*
Laurence Sterne	*Manfred Pfister*
Tom Stoppard	*Nicholas Cadden*
The Tempest	*Gordon McMullan*
Tennyson	*Seamus Perry*
Derek Walcott	*Stewart Brown*
John Webster	*Thomas Sorge*
Edith Wharton	*Janet Beer*
Women Playwrights of the 1980s	*Dimple Godiwala*
Women Romantic Poets	*Anne Janowitz*
Women Writers of Gothic Literature	*Emma Clery*
Women Writers of the 17th Century	*Ramona Wray*
Women Writers of the Late 19th Century	*Gail Cunningham*